Sunset

Remodeling Your Home

By the Editors of Sunset Books and Sunset Magazine

Lane Publishing Co., Menlo Park, California

A house in transition

Updating, altering, and making a house your *home* may be an ongoing project or one all-out effort. Regardless of the approach, you've probably found a need for ideas and information.

To help, we've looked at hundreds of remodeling solutions and selected a variety of the most useful ideas for inclusion in this book. For the transition from old to new, we've gone from A to Z: additions (pages 26-29) to zoning ordinances (page 12). There's help for children's rooms (pages 74-75) as well as kitchens (pages 80, 86-94), ceilings (pages 40-41), floors (pages 42-43), and everything in between.

For your visual stimulation, many ideas are shown in color photographs and others in detailed sketches. They're the inspiration of the people whose talents contributed to this book. To these architects, designers, and homeowners we give our appreciation. Thanks also go to Rick Morrall and Donald E. Johnson.

Supervising Editor: Dorothy Krell

Research and Text: Karen A. Paulsen

Design: Alan May

Illustrations: Clyde Foles

Cover: Photographed by Darrow M. Watt

Editor, Sunset Books: David E. Clark

Third Printing January 1981

Do some creative remodeling *of even the smallest corner of a room, and you, too, could have as pleasant an area as the one sketched here and pictured on our cover. It was originally designed as a meal planning center—yet it turned out to be much more. The desk/counter, of the same laminated wood as the bench, is used for informal dining, extra counter space, and office. Building out around the window provided compartmented space for books, plants, a telephone, recessed lighting, and enclosed storage. (For a close-up of the window, see page 17.) Rough-sawn cedar adds warm wood tones to walls, sloping ceiling, and trim. Architects: Levorsen & Cohen.*

Contents

Previewing Your Needs

Translating needs into ideas and into action

Remodeling a home is an activity that promises great personal satisfaction. Well planned and carefully carried through, remodeling can prove to be a good investment. But more important, it can meet many of your most important living needs:

• *You need more space.* Providing room for a growing family or growing interests without moving to a larger house may mean adding or expanding a room or even adding a second story.

• *You want to update.* Perhaps you've long wanted a more modern kitchen or bathroom, a house that was open to the outdoors, or a higher light level.

• *You wish to convert space.* If a third bedroom is not being used, it might be changed into a den or dining room. Space might be found in the attic to add an extra bath.

• *You'd like to rehabilitate an old house.* Though it might be almost unlivable by today's standards, an old home sometimes provides more space and charm than a contemporary dwelling. It may also have historical interest or offer the advantages of established landscaping.

Your home should be a pleasant place to relax, focus on yourself, and escape from outside pressures. For some, home is also a work place or a showplace. The purpose of this book is to help you to create an environment—a home that works for you.

Throughout the book you will find numerous sketches and photographs of ideas to consider for your remodeling. Hopefully, they'll start you thinking and help you in your decision-making. Other idea-filled *Sunset* books on building, remodeling, and home design are listed on the back cover.

Step-by-step preparation

There are certain basic steps you should take when preparing to remodel:

Evaluate what you have. What do you like about your home? What does it lack? Are rooms being used for their original purpose? Is storage your problem?

It's a good idea to inspect your house closely. Take a hard look at what you already have in the way of space. For example, do you really need an addition when the upstairs is never used?

Examine the structure of your house. On page 6 you will find brief descriptions of the structural elements in a house. Use these, and the sketch on page 7, to help you with this important step.

Ask other questions: Do you have to replace an old window, or could you give the same window a new trim, updating it and allowing you to spend your dollars elsewhere? Would recessed lighting and updated electrical systems improve the feeling in your home? Will you be able to incorporate the old with the new?

Consider saving and reusing wood doors, wood flooring, windows, and hardware. You can find other recycling hints on pages 64, 65, 68, and 69.

Remember that most buildings are products of their times. Many architects have put their own unmistakable signatures on the houses they've designed. The moldings in your home may be unique—the carpenter's own special contribution. There may even be ceiling decoration worth preserving. Indeed, you may find that you are more than satisfied to continue with the style that was originally intended for your home.

If your house has a really distinct architectural history justifying a return to its original style, you may want to consult books, documents, and publications on historic preservation. They will tell you how to remodel *backward* to restore a house to its original style.

Evaluate what you want. It may become necessary to eliminate a house's original style and achieve a different, modern one. It's even acceptable to use two totally dissimilar architectural styles in one building—a practice called "collision architecture." For instance, a steel and glass addition on a multiwindowed saltbox house can be surprisingly successful.

Consider how remodeling may affect the value of your house. Your project could price you above the resale value of homes in the area. A realtor may be able to help you estimate how much your remodeling plans will increase your home's selling price.

Consolidate and sketch. Begin to consolidate your remodeling ideas by gathering and listing your needs and desires. From magazines and books, clip the ideas and pictures that appeal to you. You'll want to show these clippings to any professionals you may hire. Seeing them will help an architect or designer to understand your taste and come up with designs you'll like.

Now take a pad of paper and sketch out your ideas

by using the circle method shown below. This method can be helpful whether you are updating a game room wall or building an addition larger than the original structure. Sketch each idea by drawing separate or overlapping circles that represent areas. Place the circles in relation to one another.

In the illustrated example, the major reason for remodeling was the need for more space, so the planners decided on an addition. The parents wanted a new bedroom away from their growing teenagers (the old bedroom would convert to a study). The teenagers wanted a rec room. Another bathroom was a must.

The first attempt at the circle design reveals a major flaw in the proposed new addition. The parents would not escape teenage noise if their new bedroom were located next to the new rec room. Clearly, an alternative design is necessary.

In the second sketch, a better solution presents itself. The old bedroom converts into the rec room, and the new addition houses the parents' bedroom suite, including a den-study and a new bath.

The third sketch provides more detail by plotting the traffic flow and the best positioning of doorways.

Envision your sketched ideas. Try to predict the traffic patterns that will develop. Will work areas, such as the kitchen, now become walk-through areas? Will noise levels be different in the new sections? Will privacy be preserved or attained? Check the path of the sun—will the new and old areas receive enough or too much light?

Keep these considerations in mind for a few weeks. As time goes by, eliminate any unworkable part of the schemes.

Then start again from scratch. Try a totally different approach. Does the new approach hold up as well as the first one? Are some ideas more workable? Try a third scheme. This process may lead to innovative solutions to your problem. Sometimes the ideas won't work, but it's better to err now on paper than later after construction starts.

Decisions, decisions, decisions

Once into remodeling, you'll face a series of major and minor choices. All of the decisions are yours to make—from the amount of money you can afford to spend to the color of trim paint you wish to select. One very important decision involves determining who will do the actual planning and work.

The section called "Getting the work done" (pages 8–11) should help you select the professionals who can best guide you, but it is you who will have to live with the results. If, in the remodeling process, you make a wrong decision or feel you've been pushed into a compromise solution, stop work and begin rethinking. It is better to do this than live with one mistake that could make the whole project undesirable.

The design and the material you use should meet *your* needs—you shouldn't have to adapt your needs to the available material or a less-than-perfect design.

Even so, you may benefit from modifying—or postponing—some plans. If a skylight will really make the difference between *just* a room and a *fantastic* room, but money is getting tight, do without the new couch you had planned. Don't skimp by buying a cheap version of the couch—you'll just be unhappy later. Sometimes it's possible to come up with a livable and humorous stopgap—an example of this might be to put up sheets with supergraphic letters spelling out "shutters to come" when the shutters you really want are back-ordered or beyond your present budget.

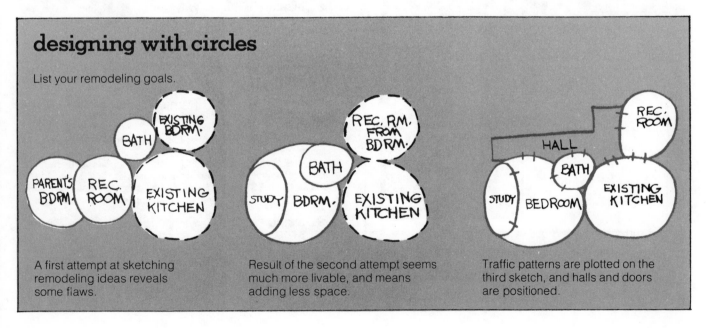

designing with circles

List your remodeling goals.

A first attempt at sketching remodeling ideas reveals some flaws.

Result of the second attempt seems much more livable, and means adding less space.

Traffic patterns are plotted on the third sketch, and halls and doors are positioned.

House Structure

Wise homeowners intent on remodeling take time to get acquainted with their house structure. The knowledge gained may be the key to much cost saving.

Before you begin any major project, for example, it is crucial to know the difference between a bearing wall—one that carries part of the weight of the house—and a nonbearing wall. It's possible that the wall you plan to tear down to create more space may be load-bearing. Of course, you can remove a bearing wall if you support the load by other means. But a less expensive solution to the space problem might be achieved by removing a nonbearing wall instead. Before you decide to remove any wall, however, you must consider what wires or pipes might be contained in that wall.

Speaking of pipes—a new bathroom, if placed near existing water supply and drain pipes, may require only quick, uncomplicated connections. If a bath is planned away from the existing plumbing, though, the added hookup expense will be considerable.

Even if you do not plan to do the detailed inspection yourself, become familiar with the house structure and terms illustrated here. When dealing with professionals, you will find it helpful to know some of their basic terminology. See page 12, too, for some symbols used in architectural drawings and blueprints.

here are your house "bones"

BEARING WALL. Partition that supports a floor or roof above. Generally, bearing walls are perpendicular to the ceiling joists or beams, and parallel to the roof ridge.

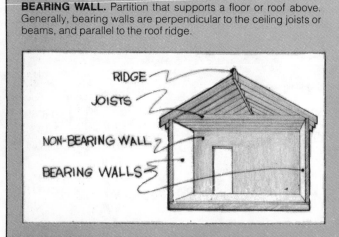

RIDGE
JOISTS
NON-BEARING WALL
BEARING WALLS

NONBEARING WALL. Partition that supports its own weight but no other load.

1. **ATTIC FLOORING.** Wood strips or plywood laid on top of ceiling joists.
2. **BEARING POST.** Steel or wood post used to support a load above.
3. **BRIDGING.** Short wooden blocks (possibly "X" angled) or metal bars used for bracing between joists.
4. **BUILDING FELT** (sheathing paper). Asphalt-impregnated paper used on walls, floors, ceilings, or roofs to provide a moisture barrier.
5. **COLLAR BEAMS** (collar ties). Braces that connect the rafters on opposite sides of a roof.
6. **CRIPPLE STUDS.** Studs that are shorter than others in a wall; for example, cripple studs are used under a window opening.
7. **DIAGONAL CORNER BRACES.** Diagonal boards notched into or fitted between studs to keep a wall square and give it lateral support; recently thin metal strips have come into use to replace boards.
8. **EAVES.** Rafter overhang at the lower edge of a roof.
9. **FIRE STOPS.** Horizontal blocking between wall studs that helps to prevent the internal spread of fire.
10. **FLASHING.** Noncorrosive sheet metal used for seepage protection at joints subject to water penetration.
11. **FOUNDATION.** The support on which a structure rests.
12. **FURRING.** Strips of wood or metal applied to a wall, ceiling, or floor to level it for a finished covering material.
13. **GIRDER.** Large horizontal beam of wood or steel used to support other parts of a structure.
14. **GUTTER.** Shallow channel set along the eaves of a house to carry rainwater from the roof.
15. **HEADERS. (a)** Horizontal wood beam placed directly above an opening such as a window or door. **(b)** Joist-size timber nailed to the ends of a series of joists.
16. **INSULATION.** Material highly resistant to heat gain or loss in a structure. (See page 59.)
17. **INTERIOR FINISH.** Material used to cover inside framed areas, such as walls, ceilings, and floors.
18. **JOISTS.** Series of parallel beams laid edgewise to support floors and ceilings and supported in turn by beams, girders, bearing walls, or foundations.
19. **PARTITION STUDS.** Studs in a wall that subdivides spaces within a story.
20. **PIER.** Column of masonry resting on a footing or on the ground and serving as a foundation for other structural members.
21. **PLATES. (a)** Sill plate or mud sill. Lowest member of a frame structure that rests on the foundation. **(b)** Top plate. Two horizontal members above the studs of a frame wall supporting ceiling joists and rafters. **(c)** Bottom plate or sole plate. Bottom horizontal member of a frame wall.
22. **RAFTERS.** Series of sloping members that make up the framework that supports the roof. (Rafters of a flat roof are called roof or ceiling joists.)
23. **RIDGE BOARD.** Central framing member at the peak of a roof to which the rafters are fastened.
24. **SHEATHING.** Wide boards or plywood (used over studs or rafters of a structure) to which roofing or siding is attached.
25. **SHINGLES.** Roof or wall coverings of asphalt, asbestos, slate, tile, wood, or other material applied in an overlapping manner.
26. **SIDING.** Exterior wall covering, usually of a wooden material.
27. **STUDS.** Upright vertical members that provide a framework for wall materials and support the overhead structure.
28. **SUBFLOOR.** Boards or plywood laid across joists over which a finished floor is laid.

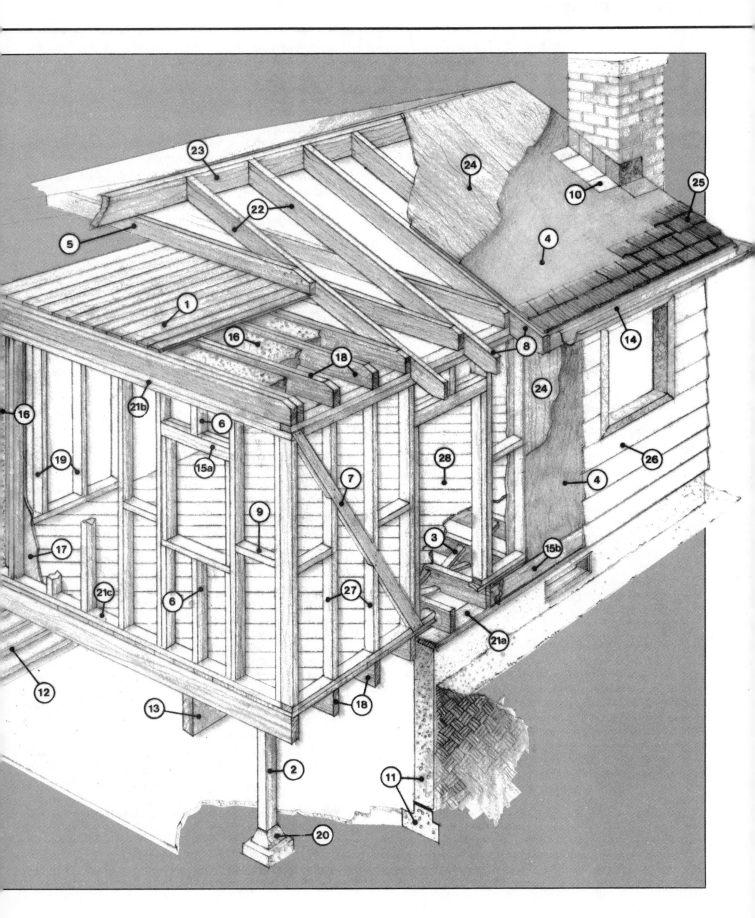

Getting the Work Done

Whether your remodeling project calls for simply installing a stained glass window in a bathroom or lavishly adding a grand ballroom, you're likely to need some professional guidance. The trick is to decide which kind of advice to seek.

Your choice in professionals

The guide that follows gives brief introductions to the professionals whose services you may find useful.

Architects are usually chosen when esthetics and detailing are particularly important or when there are special design problems.

In addition to organizing your basic needs and making rough sketches of practical solutions, an architect can

• draw up precisely detailed plans and specifications for bids

• ensure that nothing contradicts local codes and ordinances (the contractor usually handles permits in remodeling)

• provide working drawings and specifications to the contractor

• supervise the contractor's work

• check handiwork, time schedules, and grades of materials

• make the final inspection of the completed work

• sign a certificate of approval when both of you are completely satisfied.

You can also hire an architect on a one-time, hourly basis for advice on a particular part of your remodeling project. If you want to do the construction or supervise the building yourself, you can hire an architect to do only the designing, working drawings, and specifications.

Interior decorators and designers provide help that ranges from traditional decorator's recommendations for upholstery fabrics, wallpapers, carpeting, and furniture to complete room designs. They are experts at making sense out of that drawerful of clippings you may have preserved.

Complete designs give specifications for built-ins, fixtures, and appliances, as well as recommendations for structural change. Be certain, though, that the person giving recommendations of a structural nature is qualified to do so. Some members of the American Society of Interior Designers pass a qualifying examination for this.

Building designers, usually licensed by the state, are often hired when the remodeling project is straightforward or is a basic addition of space, such as a bedroom and bath.

Draftspeople incorporate your final design ideas into plans you can use when asking for contractors' bids and applying for building permits.

General contractors handle all phases of home remodeling by

• working with the architect, designer, or homeowner in meeting specifications for materials and construction

• hiring subcontractors for specific phases of the project and coordinating their work

• setting work sequence and schedules

• securing all needed building permits and inspections

• purchasing all materials and supplies

• furnishing tools and equipment.

Subcontractors are your best bet if you have specific jobs to be done. Hire those contractors who are equipped to offer you expert and specialized service in painting, plumbing and heating, air conditioning, roofing and siding, electrical work, masonry, paving, storm windows and screens, fencing, insulation, exterminating, and landscaping.

Checking out professionals

When you set out to find and hire a professional to guide you in remodeling your home, be as careful and selective as you would be in choosing a doctor, a lawyer, or a babysitter. The relationship is an intimate one, involving matters of personal taste and life style.

It's wise to get names and recommendations from friends, neighbors, business associates, trade associations, material suppliers, or real estate brokers. Other valuable sources are books, magazines, and the Yellow Pages of your telephone book. For further assistance you can contact professional associations, such as the American Institute of Architects (AIA) or the American Society of Interior Designers (ASID).

Contact your most promising leads and talk over your plans and budget limits with them. Look at plans and photos of work they've done. Finally, get in touch with some former clients and judge their work yourself.

If you plan to work with more than one professional, it's wise to say so as early as possible—should there be some existing incompatibilities, you may want to make a change.

Working directly with a contractor

When you decide to work directly with a contractor, you assume a fair amount of responsibility.

Verify references. Here are some questions to ask when checking references: Was the price quoted in

During a remodeling project *a work area may be hazardous, with scattered tools, dust, and debris. Workers in your home, noise, lack of water and electricity—all may be part of the project; in some instances you may even have to move out. Being prepared for these situations is the first step in making your remodeling easier to get through.*

Worth-it-all result: *A luxurious one-room bath remodeled from a dressing room and small bath. It's well illuminated with a series of downlights and skylights. Walls, ceiling, and vanity are faced with tongue-and-groove clear cedar, and the vanity top and tub facings are marble. The mirror wall conceals storage and visually widens the room.*

Architect-designed circular staircase is a highlight in this home. The stairs are of 2 by 4s that radiate outward. They're notched into and bolted to a stained utility pole that forms the core. Thick rope, pulled taut through oar locks, acts as a handrail. For more about this remodel, see page 28. Architect. Roger East.

Owner-installed tile accents the risers of these original stairs. To completely redo the stairs would have meant bringing them up to code. Instead, the owners decided on a decorative touch. For added interest, they chose a different tile pattern for each level, and the result is quite refreshing.

advance, and did the contractor stick to it? Were there extra, unexpected charges? Were the owners pleased with the work? Was the contractor agreeable to work with? Was the project completed on schedule?

Have your bank or savings and loan association check the contractor's financial responsibility. You can get verification of the currency and validity of the contractor's license from the state licensing board. The contractor's insurance agent can tell you if the certificate of public liability and property damage insurance is current.

If you have further doubts, check with your community's Better Business Bureau. These organizations keep files of any negative information given to them within the last 3 years.

Solicit several bids. It is customary to invite two or three competitive bids on a project. Contractors have several ways of bidding a project. You should have them break down costs to help you make a decision about the best building plan or selection of materials. Be somewhat leery of a bid that is considerably lower than the others—the finished job may end up being a slipshod one.

Check bonding and lien protection. Find out to what extent the contractor is bonded. (Normally, if a job is not completed, the bond is forfeited.) If the cost of your project exceeds the contractor's bonding capabilities, make sure that each of your payments (usually there are four or five) is just less than the costs to date—so that if work stops, you won't lose heavily.

Under the laws of most states, anyone who performs labor or supplies materials for a building can file a lien against the building if he or she is not paid. If the contractor does not settle the claim, the building's owner may be liable even though the contractor has received full payment. Lien laws do vary from state to state so you should consult your attorney to determine the best way to protect yourself.

Obtain a contract. A detailed contract should list specifications for all materials, appliances, and structural components; it should also specify completion schedules, total costs, and method of payment. If you plan to do some of the work yourself, this should also be spelled out.

Once you have hired a contractor, be prepared for work to begin. Have furniture, carpets, and drapes out of the way when workers arrive.

Keep a close eye on the work and the materials being used, but do not get in the way. Avoid giving any direct instructions to the employees; always deal with them through the contractor.

After the job is completed and you are satisfied with it, address a formal letter of acceptance to the contractor, who will then file a completion notice with the county recorder's office. If the work is unsatisfactory, however, withhold payment until the job is satisfactory.

If you join in the work

Your desires or pocketbook may dictate that you take an active role in the remodeling of your home. Having faced this reality, you may choose to do some or all of the contracting and labor yourself.

Being your own general contractor can be a seemingly endless task. You'll be in charge of coordinating all the work—getting electricians in before other workers enclose the walls, checking to see that carpenters are not sawing in an area that is being painted.

Talk with your insurance broker and state workers' compensation board before hiring help. Workers coming on the job and earning over a certain minimum wage must be covered by worker's compensation insurance. If they work for a licensed subcontractor—such as a painter, electrician, or roofer—they are covered by the subcontractor's policies. But if they work for you and you pay them directly, you must carry the insurance.

For an extensive project that will involve many hours of labor, you will need to register with state and federal governments as an employer, withhold and remit income taxes and disability insurance, and pay social security and unemployment insurance costs.

You must also talk to your local building inspection department to determine whether a permit needs to be taken out and inspections made. (See the section on permits, page 12.)

Doing part of the work yourself is a matter that should be talked out before work begins. A contractor working on a bid contract isn't likely to want your assistance—your capabilities are an unknown quantity, and insurance may not cover you. Still, if a contractor is assured you won't slow down the job, he or she may agree to your doing specific tasks. Your responsibilities should be stated in the contract, and a statement included releasing the contractor from any liability for the work you perform.

Doing all the work yourself involves a multitude of responsibilities. First, you should check your property title for deed restrictions and easements. Prepare scale drawings of your house and proposed remodeling sketches to show to the building department. The building inspector will check them for violations in zoning and code restrictions. In addition, a building inspector can often help with suggestions on easier ways to solve a problem.

Given a preliminary go-ahead, you can prepare final plans and get permits. Compose a detailed materials list, do some comparison pricing, and make your purchases. You will have to arrange for financing (see page 13) and, if you hire help, obtain workers' compensation insurance and arrange for withholding taxes and social security contributions. Remember, it is your responsibility to arrange for building inspections, both during and at the end of construction.

Regulations & Finance

Your remodeling project will have to conform to certain regulations, including deed restrictions, zoning ordinances, and building codes. You will probably have to get permission to do what you plan by securing building, plumbing, and electrical permits.

Deeds, zoning, and codes protect you

The following paragraphs explain some of the regulations that might affect you in remodeling your home.

Deed restrictions are limitations on the use of property. They are usually established by the developer to maintain a level of excellence in the neighborhood, and thus stabilize property value. These restrictions can be found either in your deed or in a document filed in the local recording office.

Read your deed carefully for limitations before starting any remodeling project. It may restrict the style of architecture, materials used, or even colors of exterior paint. The deed may also specify where an addition can be placed and may restrict the construction of garages or second stories.

Zoning ordinances can be obtained from the community's building department. They define how the land and buildings can be used in areas of your community. These ordinances are meant to protect you.

Zoning ordinances ease the strain on municipal water, sewage, and other services by restricting the number of families living in one house. These ordinances also regulate maximum percent of land coverage; front, side, and back setbacks; and the heights of fences and hedges.

Building codes are meticulous standards that often may seem exasperating, but they were written for your health, safety, and protection.

Most communities have adopted the Uniform Building, Mechanical, and Plumbing Codes and the National Electrical Code with amendments for local concerns. Your library should have copies. Periodic revisions may not be adopted promptly, so ask your local building departments which editions are in use.

For your home, the codes stipulate minimum standards, quality and size of construction material, plumbing, and electrical fittings. The codes also give guidelines for the construction of some structures.

Variances to zoning and code regulations can be obtained when a literal interpretation seems impractical or illogical. A variance is usually granted if it will not be harmful to neighbors, adjacent property, or public welfare.

Remember that variances are as much a part of the law as regulations. You always have a right to present your reasons for asking that the rules be waived. Simply submit a variance application to the appropriate zoning or planning official. You will probably be asked to appear at a hearing where a ruling will be made.

There is usually an appeal process established to review variance denials. Anyone wanting to dispute a variance decision may submit relevant information to the appropriate board or official. The final authority may lie with your city council or county board of supervisors.

Permits are referred to in Section 301 of the Uniform Building Code. The Code reads, "No person, firm, or corporation shall erect, construct, enlarge, alter, repair,

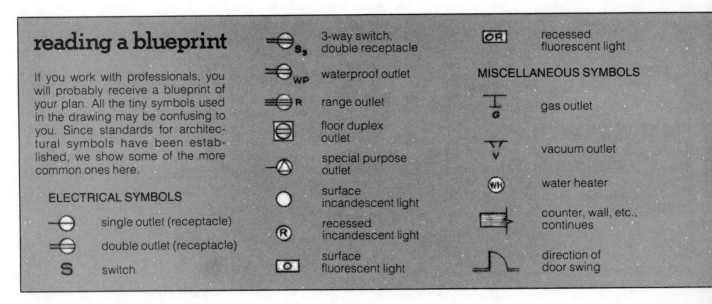

reading a blueprint

If you work with professionals, you will probably receive a blueprint of your plan. All the tiny symbols used in the drawing may be confusing to you. Since standards for architectural symbols have been established, we show some of the more common ones here.

ELECTRICAL SYMBOLS

single outlet (receptacle)

double outlet (receptacle)

S   switch

3-way switch, double receptacle

waterproof outlet

range outlet

floor duplex outlet

special purpose outlet

surface incandescent light

recessed incandescent light

surface fluorescent light

recessed fluorescent light

MISCELLANEOUS SYMBOLS

gas outlet

vacuum outlet

water heater

counter, wall, etc., continues

direction of door swing

move, improve, remove, convert, or demolish a building or structure in the city, or cause the same to be done, without first obtaining a separate building permit for each such building or structure from the Building Official."

The code covers greenhouses, patio covers, skylights, carports—almost every structural project you can think of. It would also seem to cover almost every home remodeling project. In actual practice, though, there's a little more leeway.

Permit requirements vary from one area to another, but they are seldom concerned with cabinetry, refinishing, paneling, painting, and other things that do not "alter the use" or the basic structure itself. If you don't want to risk a penalty, ask the building department about the work you intend to do. If you hire contractors, they should be responsible for obtaining necessary permits, though the responsibility is ultimately yours.

If you are doing the work yourself, discuss your ideas with a building inspector and ask for an application for a building permit. In it, you will have to
• describe the work to be done
• give the lot, block, tract, street address, or assessor's parcel number of the location
• indicate use of occupancy
• state the valuation of the new construction
• submit two to four sets of detailed plans.

Take the completed application and drawings to the building office with the required fee. Depending on the complexity of the project, you may have to apply for electrical and plumbing permits in addition to the building permit.

Some pointers on financing

Spend some time reviewing the amount of money your remodeling will cost. A rule-of-thumb is that remodeling should not exceed two-thirds the cost of a comparable new house. (In some instances, if the remodeling costs exceed one-half the value of the existing structure, the entire structure may have to be brought up to code.) When you've arrived at a realistic figure, shop around for financing. But before you actually make loan arrangements—unless it is a very small home improvement loan—be sure to have on hand finished plans and accurate estimates of work to be done.

Financing for remodeling projects can come from various sources. Where you obtain financing and the type of financing that's best for you depend primarily on how much money you need to borrow.

You can borrow from commercial banks, savings and loan associations, savings banks, mortgage bankers, credit unions, or rich relatives. Or you can borrow against your life insurance equity, refinance your present mortgage with a second mortgage, obtain advances on an open-end mortgage, or remortgage your home if the property is clear of debt.

Weigh the advantages and disadvantages of each type of loan. Naturally you'll want to obtain the lowest interest rate possible.

insurance policies should be revised to meet your home's new value. Be sure to increase the amount of your homeowner's insurance immediately, and check the insurance level periodically to see that it keeps up with inflation.

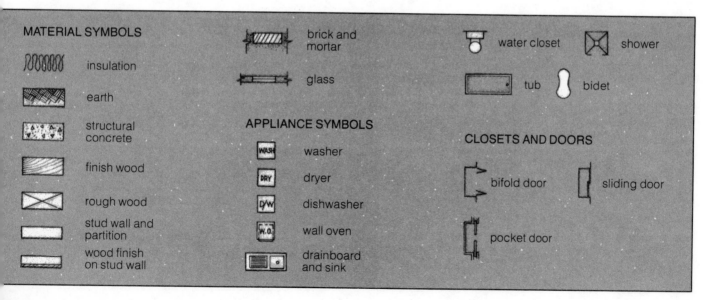

MATERIAL SYMBOLS

insulation

earth

structural concrete

finish wood

rough wood

stud wall and partition

wood finish on stud wall

brick and mortar

glass

APPLIANCE SYMBOLS

WASH — washer

DRY — dryer

D/W — dishwasher

W.O. — wall oven

drainboard and sink

water closet

shower

tub

bidet

CLOSETS AND DOORS

bifold door

sliding door

pocket door

Updating with Lighting

Illumination from windows, skylights, and artificial sources

Light is a fascinating medium. While it seems to have no shape or substance of its own, it is, nevertheless, a vital element in determining the quality of a living environment. This is true of both natural and artificial light.

Lighting experts know how to measure light and how it reflects from different colors and materials. They know, for instance, that it takes more light to brighten a darkly painted room than to light one that is painted white. The amount of light we "see" in a room is also affected by the texture of the surfaces it hits and by the degree of contrast between light and dark areas.

But personal reaction to light can't be predicted. One person may choose an evenly lighted room; another may prefer the dramatic contrast of spotlighted accent areas and shadowy corners. Lighting the home is as much a matter of taste as it is of scientific calculation.

Windows allow daylight and sunshine to enter our rooms. They provide ventilation and emergency exits. And what's more, they answer our psychological need to know the weather and what is outside.

Relocating a window can be costly, so try to work around existing windows. You may be able to enhance an old window with other treatments—deepening the sill for plant display, for instance, or building in a window seat (see page 22).

When you plan new window placements, check the path of the sun for the possibility of future glare and solar damage. For more on solar protection, see page 59.

Consider your need for privacy, too. Will your neighbors be able to see in? You may have to achieve privacy with some type of window covering—curtains, shutters, or Venetian blinds. Or perhaps you can position windows to face trees rather than a neighbor's house.

Skylights and skywindows have come a long way since the days when they were a staple of the artist's unheated garret. Bringing in natural overhead light, they can be a boon for every area in the home—especially the kitchen, bedroom, bath, and hall. See pages 20 and 21 for more on skylights.

Artificial light has effectively brightened homes since Edison invented the light bulb. A homeowner setting out to improve existing light or to light a new area is likely to be faced with many choices—among them direct, indirect, fluorescent, incandescent, spot, and track lighting. Pages 18 and 19 will help you with such choices.

levels of lighting

Windows let in natural light and allow us to see out. In daytime, a room can be used in comfort and ease with just the light from this one source.

Work surfaces are not efficient unless the light in the room lets you work without eyestrain. To eliminate shadows, there must be adequate light, properly positioned.

When you entertain, light should encourage guests to linger. Dimmed lights, highlighting spots, light from candles, and even the fireplace, set an inviting mood.

Globe lights *in the ceiling of this room plug directly into an electrical outlet strip, using every other outlet. Windows angle toward the fireplace corner, allowing tree-filtered daylight to brighten the seating areas. Shade-covered lights hang down from exposed rafters. Architect: Tim Ward.*

Window Styles

Because window treatment plays such an important role in most remodeling, we offer the sketches on the opposite page to give you an overview of the most-used window styles. Look at the color photographs for examples of imaginative window uses that leave the ordinary far behind.

These are the basic styles of windows found in most homes:

• *Fixed pane.* Good for small, irregularly shaped areas; also used when oversize view windows make movable frames impractical.

• *Sliding.* Can be used in almost any room in the house; best suited to contemporary architecture.

• *Casement.* Fits well into bay or bow windows; also lends itself to row installation.

• *Double hung.* Probably best used in older homes and with classic colonial architecture.

• *Awning.* Good for any room where ventilation is needed in rainy weather; provides privacy as a high window in a bath or bedroom.

• *Jalousie.* Most often found in bathrooms, closets, kitchens, clerestories—wherever light, privacy, and ventilation are needed.

• *Skylight.* Used to bring sunlight into a gloomy area; provides more privacy than a side window. Pages 20 and 21 cover the many variations on the skylight.

In planning for your windows, remember that size and positioning are all-important. Keep openings consistent in style, placement, and size with the existing windows. Enlarging some windows—those in attics, for example—can cause them to look out of proportion with the entire house. But if the difference in window sizes can't be controlled, don't despair—it's usually possible to offset the mismatch with color or decoration.

Greenhouse section, *cut to size and installed above the sink, is the window in this kitchen. The owners made an indentation into the overhang of the roof to accommodate the curved glass, gaining light and a view. Plants have thrived. Design: Jane and Paul Juliet.*

Large and small windows can add interest in a remodel. The window above is framed in wood and, as part of a bookcase design, is positioned above the desk (see front cover). Architects: Levorson & Cohen. The colorful leaded glass at right was owner-designed and executed. It's actually a five-panel window wall—three clear glass panels are covered with shades. Design: Jerry Clarke.

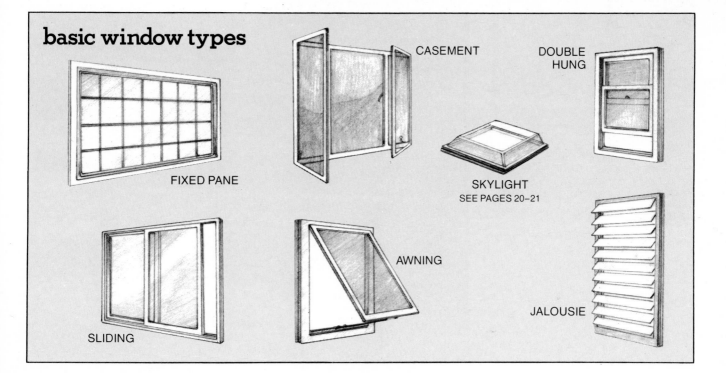

basic window types

FIXED PANE

CASEMENT

DOUBLE HUNG

SKYLIGHT
SEE PAGES 20–21

SLIDING

AWNING

JALOUSIE

Track lights, *their housings painted the same color as the surrounding walls, give added emphasis to a 10-panel Chinese mural in this room. Candlelight and the warm overall glow from a fire in the fireplace contribute soft, flattering light for entertaining. Floor and table lamps are light sources for reading.*

A special object *in your home can be effectively accentuated with light that outlines its shape. Here the light in the ceiling is directed in rectangle form on the painting by means of shields and a lens close to the light source.*

Artificial Sources

Just as a fresh coat of paint can perk up a house, so the right kind of artificial lighting can enliven a room. Well-planned lighting enhances a room's design, radiating out to create patterns and highlights. On the other hand, hit-or-miss lighting can make a room flat and dull.

Spend time deciding what sort of illumination you want. While thinking of the "big picture," remember to give attention to the "little picture," too. For example, you might include lighting for closets and storage areas, or for an area where a hobby or collection is on display. In a complex situation, you may want to consult a lighting engineer.

Study lighting in the homes and indoor areas you visit at night. Are the lights incandescent or fluorescent? Are they on dimmer switches? Is the lighting direct, indirect, or a combination? Are there luminous ceiling panels? Is the source a spotlight, track light, or chandelier? Are there table, floor, or swag lamps?

Ideally, a room should contain two types of light. One provides overall, glare-free light on floor areas and traffic paths. The other is supplemental lighting, directed or reflected to specific work areas on counters, desks, and tables; over cooktops and sinks; around mirrors.

The number of light sources is also important. This can be very much a matter of personal taste. To one person, four scattered sources may seem more effective than one large source; to another, one source may have greater impact than four.

Choices in lighting range from the conventional to something as wild as brightly colored tubes of light that vibrate when different intensities of recorded sound are played.

Track lights in a multitude of designs set on swivel fixtures put the light exactly where you want it. Since copper conductors run the entire length of the track, the lights can usually be moved to any position. One light on the track might be used for reading, the others for overall lighting.

A spot bulb, which focuses light with great intensity, makes a good reading light; floods, which spread more light in a fairly wide arc, can highlight art on the walls.

Illumination can also come from recessed downlights. The width of the beam given off by these lights will depend on the distance between each downlight and the surface receiving the illumination, as well as on the type of bulb used and on the fitting (fully recessed, semirecessed, surface mounted, or protruding). Downlights most often require at least a 12-inch space above the ceiling for their housing units.

Most people are accustomed to light sources at or above eye level. But the effect is quite different when light comes from below—it can add a new dimension to a room.

A floor light (as simple as a small high-intensity or eyeball light) placed between a chest and the wall allows light to gently wash over the wall, backlighting objects on the chest. A light directed upward to illuminate an indoor plant or tree will throw interesting shadows against the walls and ceiling.

Select the proper light bulb and container for the job. Some containers are just bulb holders; others have high sides that control the direction of light. Because a visible bulb often fatigues the eyes, try whenever possible to conceal the light source.

Dimmer switches let you dial the mood of any room—softly lighted and inviting for parties and quiet dinners, brighter for reading and work.

Dimmers can also save you money. They reduce the current reaching the bulbs. And, because they burn at a reduced temperature, light bulbs last longer.

Different types of dimmers are available: wall switches, table models, on-the-socket switches, on-the-cord types. All are easy to use—you can choose the intensity of lighting you want by merely turning a dial or moving a switch.

Heart of this family kitchen is a well-lighted 4 by 9*-foot cooking-serving-eating counter. The entire area receives light during the day from high skylights. For more specific illumination, there are track lights angled at work areas or art objects, and boxed lights pointed directly at the counter. For diffused light, still another source is shielded with translucent plastic. Architect: Paul H. Elliott.*

Skylights & Skywindows

A skylight is a practical way to bring natural light into an area where daylight is blocked off or nonexistent. Sometimes it's the only way to get more daylight into an older house without destroying the original house lines by enlarging windows.

The appeal of a skylight is that it gives depth and changing character to a room. At the same time it provides uniform lighting and privacy. With the use of different skylight styles and shaft angles, you can also direct light to suit your own purposes—to highlight a piece of sculpture or to diffuse light throughout a room.

Acrylic is the most commonly used material in skylights today. It can be clear to allow for an overhead view, or translucent to reduce glare and diffuse light.

In regions of intense sunlight, skylights can create hot spots on carpets and floors. If this is a possibility in your home, consider skylights with built-in shutters that control heat and light, or the more expensive skylights that are effectively insulated with double domes. You can also block the light below the shaft with horizontal curtains or shutters.

A translucent panel installed beneath a skylight shaft at the ceiling line diffuses light and controls heat loss. Light fixtures installed and concealed in the shaft above the panel can supply night illumination.

Here we present examples of standard skylights you can purchase for home installation, as well as some interesting adaptations of the skylight or skywindow.

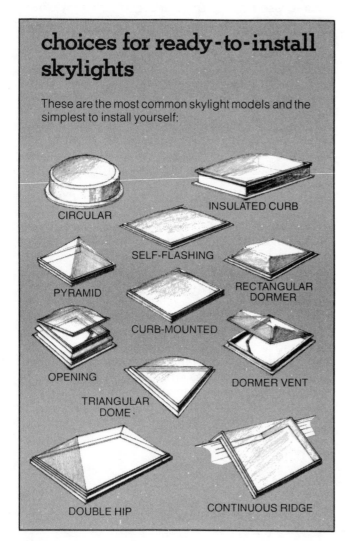

choices for ready-to-install skylights

These are the most common skylight models and the simplest to install yourself:

CIRCULAR

INSULATED CURB

SELF-FLASHING

PYRAMID

RECTANGULAR DORMER

CURB-MOUNTED

OPENING

DORMER VENT

TRIANGULAR DOME

DOUBLE HIP

CONTINUOUS RIDGE

A solarium at times, this sitting area becomes an open court when the glass "ceiling" rolls away on its garage door hardware. The roll-away sky window is made of ¼-inch-thick wire glass with a frame of redwood 2 by 4s. Design: Phil Emminger.

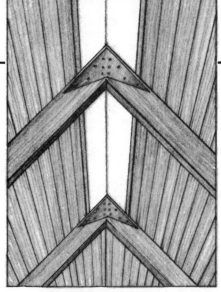

The soaring peak of an A-frame is brightened by a plastic ridge skylight. The 4 x 12-inch roof timbers angle steeply to the top, where they are bolted to metal plates. Design: The Jeffery Smiths.

A ceiling of bubble skylights brings in lots of light. In this small addition, three 4 x 8-foot acrylic skylights were used. Horizontal curtains, strung on wire under the ceiling diffuse the light. Architect: Roy Richard Ettinger.

A skylight opens up an otherwise confined space. Tile surrounds the tub and walls, as well as the sitting and plant ledge. To allow standup head room, the skylight over the sunken bath is convex. Architect: Ed Heine; Contractor: Dick York.

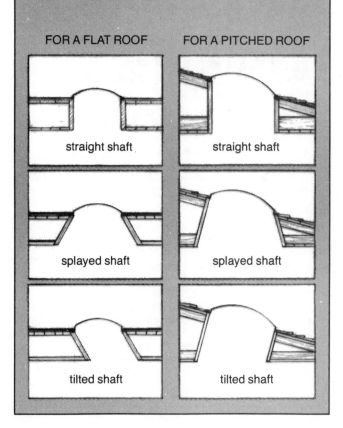

light shaft angles

Sometimes a skylight requires a shaft to tunnel in the light from outside. The shaft can be straight, or tilted to any convenient angle. Here are some examples:

FOR A FLAT ROOF   FOR A PITCHED ROOF

straight shaft   straight shaft

splayed shaft   splayed shaft

tilted shaft   tilted shaft

Window seats

Window seats can serve many needs—from creating a comfortable reading nook to providing a spot for an indoor garden.

The type and size of seat you want will determine how it is built. Part or all of a wall could be knocked out and the seat cantilevered above ground level. Or you might want to build inward from an existing window, creating a ledge surrounded by bookcases or storage. (By doing this, you could also gain some under-the-seat storage.)

When you plan your window seat, keep in mind that the seating area may not automatically have ideal light and heat. Install sufficient outlets to serve the artificial light sources you will need, and plan to screen harsh sunlight in daytime. In cold-winter areas, you may want to install a heater. Blankets or a cozy quilt provide an alternative source of warmth and comfort, and they can be kept right in the seat itself, available for spur-of-the-moment use.

Finishing touches make window seats more inviting. Upholstered cushions of 4 to 6-inch-thick foam rubber are comfortable; dacron batting wrapped around the foam makes them seem even more luxurious. An array of pillows is attractive and can enhance the decor of the room.

Large stair landings, a feature of many older homes, offer a perfect place for a window seat; a seat, in turn, gives prominence to a seldom used area. Here a dark wood seat lifts to reveal hidden storage. Leaded glass, a curving banister, and plants help to make the area inviting.

Window seat arrangement was created by a wide, comfortable couch and bookshelves built into one end of this small study. Hidden under the solid looking couch is generous storage space. The same effect can be achieved with a standard couch surrounded by shelves, thus creating a bay for the window. Architect: William Dutcher.

This skylighted retreat was tucked into the steep roof area of a second floor remodel. The alcove accommodates a single bed for guest sleeping; or with pillows added, it's a good place for sitting. Built-in bookcases with reading lights make further use of space under the sloping roof. Design: Richard W. Painter.

New Expanses from Added Space

Gaining room by putting surplus areas to use, or by adding on

The space you want to gain by remodeling may range from modest to extensive. You may have in mind permanently enclosing a small back porch—or putting on an addition twice as large as the original house. This chapter offers you some inspiration as well as the information you need to add space.

There are more space-expanding ideas throughout the book. Look especially in the boundaries chapter, beginning on page 32. You may also want to consider further ideas in the *Sunset Add-a-Room Book.*

Adding just a little space may serve your purpose well. The photographs here illustrate how even a very small additional space can give your home something extra. Pages 26–29 discuss larger additions; pages 28 and 29 deal with additions that are unusual. Ideas for "borrowing" a little bit of space are explained on pages 30 and 31.

Originally a porch on the second story, the area shown below is now part of the enclosed house—a solarium adjacent to the kitchen. The windows provide ample light for it to be used as a work room, and it's a pleasant place to eat breakfast or just enjoy the view. Architect: Robert B. Marquis of Marquis Associates.

One way to gain space is with an outdoor area that seems to be part of the house. Here a living room opens to an outdoor room above the garage. Wood and glass enclose the sides, but the top is open to the elements. Colorful leaded glass highlights the wood wall at the end, where the view is uninteresting.
Architect: Douglas Snow.

Uninterrupted panoramic view is the result of this window wall that juts out of the room and gives added space. The small window seat on the left is a cozy retreat; silicone seals the glass where it meets in this corner. Overhanging eaves form a visor for sun and rain protection.
Architect: George Cody.

The Addition

If you've decided that you need more space in your house, you're probably considering an addition. Where and how you locate that addition will be important. (See "Consolidate and sketch," page 4.) Several possibilities for placement are open to you—you can build up, out, or down—even underground. Or you may be able to add a unit that is separate from the main body of your house. Be sure to check zoning regulations first.

During the planning stages, you may want to take a picture of the exterior of your house and have it enlarged. On tracing paper overlays, sketch several possible locations, sizes, and styles of additions. If you're interested in using an unconventional shape in creating your addition, see pages 28 and 29 for some ideas.

The function of the room you are adding will play a role in determining its location. Rooms in which people are active—kitchens, playrooms, hobby rooms—are often best located on the cooler, north side of the house. Rooms to be used for sedentary activity—studies, living rooms—are well placed on the south side of a house where trapped winter sunlight can help to defray heating costs.

Also consider how many uses you want your addition to serve. Will it be one room or many? You may solve your space needs by building a versatile room that combines two or more uses. Consider a dining/garden room, a game/hobby room, or a kitchen/family room.

Consider the size of your addition very carefully. Don't build too small. If you skimp, you may always yearn for those extra few feet of floor, closet, shelf, or counter

space that would have made the difference between cramped quarters and ample space. On the other hand, don't create a monster that you won't use but will still have to clean and heat.

If you are adding on in steps, never lose sight of the long-range plans you have for your home. Try to incorporate plumbing and electrical elements in the walls for future use so that you won't have to open walls later.

Rooms need not have four solid walls. In Hawaii, homeowners often achieve an open and relaxed concept of space with a *lanai*—a veranda, porch, or living room that's open in part to the outdoors. Despite the relatively harsher climates of the mainland, lanais may be used with success. Sliding or folding glass doors can close off the outside portion of the room to inclement or cold weather. The doors can open wide to admit sun and refreshing breezes in warmer months. For another idea with similar advantages, see the outdoor living area shown at the top of page 25.

Do some checking on standard-size materials for your addition. Planning around such stock items as 4 by 8-foot plywood, modular cabinets, and standard sliding glass doors can save you money and eliminate waste. See what stock items will fit into your plans. They are generally less expensive than those that are custom made.

Also check to be sure that your heating and cooling devices can handle the extra load of the addition. Added space, rooms with high or vaulted ceilings, and large expanses of window put more stress on these mechanical systems.

The exterior of your house will often be affected by your addition. See the section on windows in the lighting chapter of this book, pages 14–17, for some hints on window placement and size.

Think about your landscaping, too. You may want to use plants to create a feeling of cohesiveness between the old and new sections of your house. Trees and shrubs located at varying distances from the house can help create a feeling of unity between the two sections.

Consider doing some landscaping even before starting construction. If the plantings can be out of the way of—or protected from—construction workers, new bushes and trees can be growing during the actual construction. They will have made a head start by the time building is completed, and they'll help mask the raw look of a new addition.

mall but light-filled, this addition was made possible by tock greenhouse windows. The owners describe it as a vonderful room for morning coffee, afternoon naps, ighttime stargazing. The sun warms the area all year, nd there's plenty of ventilation from the window vents at ne top. The extra room is at the end of the kitchen ictured on page 16. Design: Jane and Paul Juliet.

Different Ways to Go

Additions shown in books, magazines, and other publications may offer just the spark you need to begin creative planning. You're unlikely to find the exact design for your circumstances, but you'll see ideas you like, and chances are they can be adapted to your needs.

The examples presented here go one step further than the usual. One addition was built between two existing structures. Another addition spans the original house without support from the house's foundation. In the third example, the roof was raised, saving the considerable expense of constructing a new one.

Because the slab foundation of the original house wouldn't support a second story, the architect came up with an unusual solution for an addition. He designed an independent "bridge" that spans the flat roof and is supported on treated poles that have their own separate foundation. The addition doesn't rest on the original structure at all, but is actually 18 inches above it. Access is by way of the circular staircase pictured on page 10. Architect: Roger East.

Empty space between the house and a small laundry provided enough room for a pleasant breakfast area. The old kitchen opens directly into the new glass-ceilinged area; the laundry became storage for the new room. A deck, level with the addition, helps unify the three areas. In your home you may find the same type of space available between house and garage. Architect: Clement Chen.

crane lifted the garage roof (left) like a giant wing and set aside. Next, carpenters completed flooring, studs, and racing for a teenage retreat. The crane then returned to lift e gabled roof into its new position. If you're considering a milar project, check with an experienced contractor on hether your roof is adequately braced to take the strain of e lift.

trying on your addition

Before and during construction, you may have the opportunity to actually get the *feel* of your addition. The two families shown here experienced their additions in two separate ways.

Building a paper room right where the new room would go helped this family visualize their addition before they actually broke ground. Following their architect's preliminary sketches, they stapled 4-foot-wide newsprint on a framework of old 2 by 4s. They could change windows and walls by simply cutting paper and restapling for on-the-spot designing.

This family wanted room for music. Not lacking ideas or energy, the owners set out to build their music room by themselves. After the foundation and flooring were in, they gave themselves the luxury of trying it out. Quintet and listener fit just fine.

Space Borrowing

We call it space borrowing—taking space from one area or purpose and giving it to another. It's taking the space at the top of an A-frame and making it into a bedroom loft. It's having a counter on one side of a wall and a flush, built-in stereo on the other side. It's having a second-story den look out over a two-story living room, sharing the open space. It's building a bookcase into a room but giving access to the books from the hall instead of from the room.

Look around for the many other possibilities in your home. Or you may find these space borrowing ideas so intriguing you'll duplicate one or more of them in your own remodeling plans.

Each side of this freestanding partition borrows space from the other side. The front of the divider acts as a headboard and has a lighted niche for books and other objects. The opposite side forms a dressing area with built-in drawers. Architects: Bogard and Hewitt.

Two areas in this split-level second story benefit from exchanging some space. The playroom on the left gains a child's cave, and the small amount of space borrowed from the right bedroom forms the platform for its bed loft. The wall dividing the two rooms is nonbearing. Architect: Edward Carson Beall and Associates.

Home office was gained by use of under-stair space. A bifold angled door easily opens to reveal the desk and shelves. A file cabinet fits neatly in its own closet under the stair landing. When not in use, the area can be closed off. Architect: George Cody. Associate: William Smart.

Your Room Boundaries

Working with walls, floors, ceilings, and doors

Certain structural items in a house make up its interior boundaries—walls, floors, ceilings, doors, and windows. They divide space, limit or extend the view, and give a sense of height or confinement.

The ways those boundaries are placed and treated give your house its particular character. Imagine a room: it has a door and a window; the ceiling and walls are light, the floor is dark. If it seems a little dull, let's see what we can do to make it more distinctive.

First, open the wall on one side of the room to reveal hidden storage. Next, texture the plaster on the other walls. Then, in the center of the room, sink the floor for a conversation pit and define it with a half wall. Whitewash the ceiling's wood planks; replace the window's conventional panes with beveled and leaded glass. Finally, embellish the door with molding.

The result: a striking room tailored to individual taste and needs.

This chapter offers you more food for thought concerning your house's boundaries. We dealt with windows in the chapter on lighting; here we concentrate on walls, ceilings, floors, and doors. As an introduction, let's consider ways to enliven them with color and dimension.

Color brightens up or tones down boundaries. Selecting colors may be the hardest remodeling decision you will have to make. As a rule, you will be most comfortable if you select colors from your wardrobe and apply

Defining space, yet giving a feeling of openness between rooms, these plywood-sheathed colonnades replace a series of walls that once formed the core of this Victorian house. The camera is situated in the dining room—a service porch originally, now enclosed to serve a new function. Design: Ray Kennedy.

Boundary treatment here is functional. Two areas — bath and bedroom — are defined by a partial wall and the built-in cabinet and sinks. A half-wall provides a private corner for the toilet. Ceiling, walls, and cabinet are faced with the same wood, giving continuity. Because the tile tub and plant enclosure are recessed below floor level, the room appears more spacious than it is. Large windows and a glass door extend the vision outward.
Architect: Steve Wisenbaker.

Removing the ceiling between stories was the key to creating a single spacious apartment from the two back units, home for the owners of this four-unit building. The result is an art gallery/circulation area, well lighted by the new skylight installed above the second floor. An upstairs bedroom and hallway look into the two-story gallery and share the open space. *Architect: Thomas Higley.*

Two-level ceiling of this dining room is formed by the roof line and the large soffit surrounding the outer edge; indirect light adds depth and interest. Sliding glass doors along both sides of the room give access to deck and pool, and the end window makes the most of the view. *Architect: Ellis Jacobs.*

them to your living areas. Most people intuitively select clothing colors that best complement them—our rooms should do the same.

Choose colors to suit the mood of a room. Bright colors are trendy and vibrant. Neutral tones (beiges, grays, off-whites) are the soothing classics. Variations in color and tone can also be used to delineate areas and boundaries (structural or not) or change the proportions of a room.

Colors also affect our reaction to temperatures. Certain colors can make us feel hot or cold. You can "cool" a hot south exposure with ice blue, "warm" a cold north exposure with bright yellow.

Textures in our rooms add interest. Flat walls gain prominence when paneled in wood or textured with plaster. Edges and openings that are rounded bespeak an architectural style quite different from one in which everything is finished in a sleek and angular style. Scale is achieved with bold furniture in a large room or a raised ceiling in a room that's too small.

Moldings can add prominent dimensions to boundaries, and they've been around for a long time. Their use in architecture predates ancient Greece. Even in colonial America, heavily ornate molding styles were used. Since then they have been simplified, streamlined, and even eliminated; modern design features straight, clean, bold lines.

But molding can still add eye appeal, warmth, and distinction. An interesting cove or crown molding can glamorize a plain room with minimal expense. Molding strips can easily decorate an undistinguished door; chair guards along the wall can be an architectural focal point.

Now turn the page to a chapter filled with examples of moving, lowering, raising, sinking, and eliminating walls, ceilings, and floors. In addition, you'll find coverings and treatments for boundaries; ideas for wall storage and built-ins; information on door types and styles.

There's built-in seating for six in this tiled and cushioned sunken conversation pit. Sinking the floor for your remodel may simply mean lowering floor joists, provided there is still sufficient crawl space below. Other situations may be more complicated—check with your building inspector. Architect: John S. Nance.

Moving Walls

Many interior room boundaries can change dramatically. Remove interior walls, and two small rooms become one large room. Gut an entire house, and space can be divided in a totally different way. Take special care, though, with bearing walls (see pages 6 and 7), and consult an architect or structural engineer before proceeding with any major project.

But a wall doesn't have to be eliminated altogether. By removing the top half of a wall to open up a partial view of an adjoining room, you gain a feeling of spaciousness. Half walls borrow light from another area but still screen for privacy. They direct and separate foot traffic, block drafts, and provide a backdrop for furniture.

Exterior walls have another way to go—outward. Pushing out the side of the house will open up a room, whether the wall moves a little or a lot.

Building out under the eaves of the house can be a minor change if you're able to use an existing post-and-beam support system. Here the wall moves out to the edge of the roof overhang; the few inches gained are used for extra seating and storage. Design: Rick Morrall.

A rerouting of traffic through the house can be the reason for a new corridor. Here a wall of the house was pushed out 6 feet—past the old outdoor brick barbecue and chimney. The double-sided fireplace and the new wall form a path away from living areas. (For indoor barbecuing, chimney height may need to be increased to improve the draw. Check with your building inspector for safety precautions if you want to do indoor charcoaling—charcoal fumes can be deadly.) Design: Bob Stoecker.

Half walls enclose this conversation area. People can see over, artwork has its place. Space is defined, yet the area seems large and open. With escalating building costs, lowering the walls is a good way to make a smaller house seem larger.
Architect: Antonio Attolini Lack.

Previously uninteresting, this wall was pushed out to gain light and space. Starting high on a two-story house or using the one-story slanted roof line, a wall of windows that continues on up the angled ceiling allows sunlight to spill across the room. Nighttime lighting comes from overhead lights and recessed lights under the narrow tiled counter. Architect: Harley Jensen.

Nonwalls

Nonwalls are wall-like boundaries that define an area and usually perform a function, but are not considered true walls. They exist in many homes—as storage partitions, counters, and fireplace room dividers, for example.

Another form of nonwall is the inglenook, a corner by the fireplace that has often been used most ingeniously as a high-backed seat in front of the fire to keep the warmth more concentrated. Popular in the days of unheated houses, it is now making a comeback, updated as the modern fireplace conversation pit. One more good example of creative nonwalls is the closet screen pictured on page 73.

In this section we show an array of creative nonwalls, in hopes they'll be an inspiration in your remodeling.

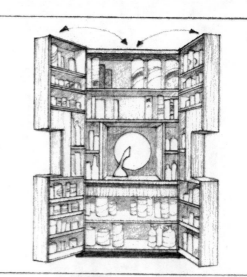

This bold divider is called a "pantry armoire" the architect, a "plethora" by the owners. forms one side of the kitchen's boundary. Whe the doors on the kitchen side are opened, as the sketch, a profusion of space for food storag is revealed; when they're closed, the circul cutout lets the cook see through to the livin room. The side facing the living room appea as a sculptured shadow box, screening t kitchen. Architect: William Turnbu

A barn door serves as a second-story wall, giving privacy at night. Then it slides away during the day so the room above shares the spaciousness of the room below. The downstairs also benefits from the lofty feeling created out of a modest square footage. For more on barn doors, see pages 55 and 57. Architect: Howard Grant.

An adaptation of the inglenook is shown here as seating next to the fireplace. Removing cushions from one end gives access to storage below. Openings pierce the walls that surround the seat, allowing for easy conversation to another room and providing a plant display area. Design: Tom Hubka and Frances Downing.

Headboard for this cantilevered bed is a different type of nonwall. On the bed side it separates the main room from the dressing area; on the other side it encloses a dresser, which is convenient to the wardrobe located behind the louvered doors. Side wing walls extend far enough into the room to provide a more intimate space for the head of the bed.
Design: Jerry Miller.

Boards face *more than the ceiling in this dining room—they continue partially down the wall to where a mirror adds visual depth to the area. To make a similar angle or a curve for your own remodel, attach straight or rounded nailing blocks to studs and joists where they meet at the corner. Nail the finishing wood to ceiling joists, corner blocks , and wall studs. Architect: William Bruder.*

Ceiling Treatments

Ceilings are often overlooked when remodeling ideas are being considered. But an unusual ceiling treatment can add a strong note of drama to an area or room.

Have you thought about painting bold supergraphics on your child's ceiling? Or using patterned wallpaper to hide unsightly ceiling cracks? How about stenciling flowers on exposed beams? Or extending an unusual wall treatment onto the ceiling?

Sometimes the answer is structural—for instance a dropped acoustical ceiling that is a twofold blessing, hiding defects, new wiring, plumbing, and ducts while absorbing noise.

Or you might consider removing a ceiling altogether, exposing beams and opening a room to a new loftiness.

Thinking of a sunken tub on the second floor? Lower the ceiling in the living room below, delineating space for an intimate game area. (First check your local building codes for minimum ceiling heights and structural considerations.)

Rooms that are to be used in daylight benefit from a light ceiling color; those primarily used at night become more cozy with a darker ceiling.

When putting on a new addition, match the old and the new ceilings to give your additional space a feeling of continuity.

Exposed ceiling joists that remain after the ceiling level has been raised are often scarred. They can be cosmetically faced with 1 by 8s and 1 by 4s. As shown here, exposed roof rafters are covered with boards to form a new lofty ceiling. Sometimes old ceiling joists can be successfully removed or repositioned; check first with a structural engineer, architect, or city building inspector. Design: Stan Jones.

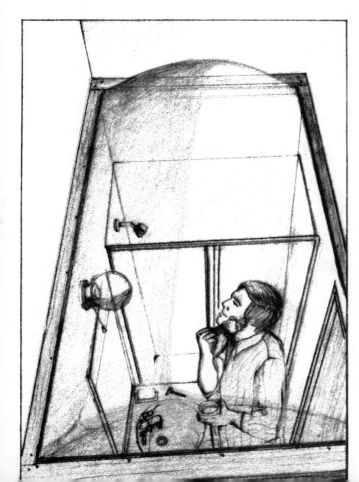

A small interior area with its own ceiling can be built into a room that has an exceptionally high ceiling. This new bath used standard 8-foot walls topped with a plexiglass bubble. Natural light from surrounding windows can penetrate the area, giving a larger feeling inside. Architect: John Schmid.

Floor Treatments

*Bathtubs are among items that "sink" well. This one with its 4-inch-high side was sunk into the crawl space; tile gives rich detailing and provides a headrest. Items placed on the floor are within easy reach of the bather.
Architect: William Churchill.*

Time was that you could look down at the floor and tell what room you were in—tile in the bath, linoleum in the kitchen. Not so today. Tile has come out from the bath to the living room. In the kitchen, plain linoleum has been replaced by more decorative flooring. High-gloss, no-wax floors now appear throughout the house. Approximately 30 types of floor coverings are available in hundreds of variations.

Here are some favorite floors, some imaginative treatments, and a structural idea:

Hardwood floors can be tongue-and-groove, parquet, parquet tile, plank, strip, or router designed.

Resilient flooring comes in rolls or sheets of vinyl, tiles of asphalt (grainy, porous surface), solid vinyl tiles (pattern penetrates full depth), vinyl asbestos tiles (pattern usually does not penetrate full depth), seamless poured vinyl and polyurethane, rubber, and cork (bonded between vinyl coatings).

Nonresilient flooring possibilities include brick, slate, quarry tile, marble tile, ceramic tile (should be skid-resistant type, not smooth type used for sinks), clay tile, stone, and terrazzo.

A conversation area was created here by raising the level of the floor rather than sinking it. Floor accents include a rug on the main level, wood plank for the risers, and cushions for sitting or resting.

Carpeting is a natural. It comes patterned or plain; plush, sculptured, level loop, or shag; weather resistant; area or wall-to-wall; wool, acrylic, nylon, polyester, or olefin. Carpets even come with giant game patterns—floor checkers, chess, or backgammon.

A little imagination can generate new ideas for floor treatments. You might paint and design your own floor—coat it with a primer, draw your design, and then apply two coats of deck enamel in appropriate colors. Try something as simple as an exercise mat in the bathroom. Ingenious flooring can be achieved with bold bed sheets attached to the floor and coated with polyurethane. Recessed door mats at the back entry and tile by the front door keep snow, rain, or mud from being tracked into the main part of the house.

Changing the level of a floor can add another dimension to a room, define an area, or give a feeling of spaciousness. By sinking the floor for a conversation pit, you will gain a warm, friendly area where the whole family can gather. To improve the view through a picture window, try raising the floor. If raised in levels, the floor can provide built-in seating.

Door mats by the dozen carpet this floor. They're placed in a grid of wood which is glued to the subfloor. Thin bricks are used as a border. Mats can be removed for vacuuming and turned over or replaced as they wear. Design: The Patrick Dailys.

Stenciling as a floor treatment is having a revival. Carpets were a rare luxury few could afford in colonial America. Handpainted floorcloth conveyed the feeling of a rug without cost; eventually paint stenciled directly on the floor became popular. It is still an inexpensive and warm way to treat a floor.

43

Wall Treatments

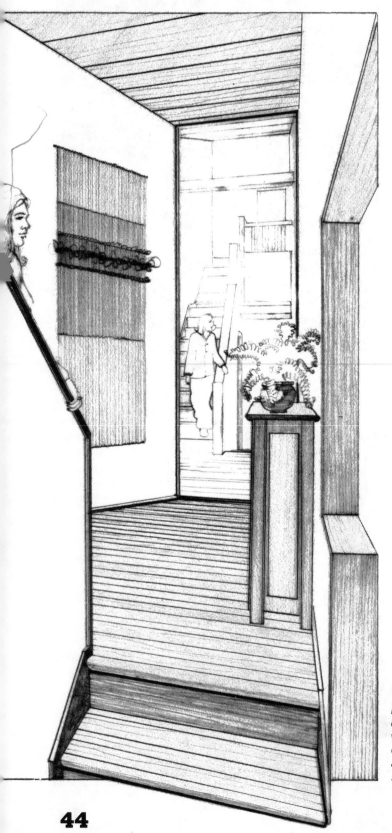

Focus on design, color, durability, and texture when you plan your wall treatments. They will play an important role in the feeling and appearance of your home.

Gypsum wallboard is by far the most widely used material—both as a finish material and as a base for other coverings—because it satisfies fire codes. Once installed and taped, it is often textured with plaster in any of a variety of ways, and then painted. Graphics, super or subtle, are an effective use of paint, giving large impact at low cost.

Wall treatments that use wallboard as a base include simulated brick, carpet, ceramic tile, stone panels, cork, glass, fabric, and wallpaper. One of our favorites for a child's room is an outline-design washable wallpaper—children just color in the design, and later the color can be washed away.

Wainscoting combines wallboard with wood or other materials. And there's also wallboard that comes predecorated with vinyl coverings.

Solid board paneling (plank) comes in many woods, but it can be as simple as scrap lumber. Planks come square edge, shiplap, tongue-and-groove, finished, unfinished, rough, smooth, "clear" (smooth, formal appearance), or "knotty" (rough, informal appearance).

Sheet paneling, such as plywood and hardboard, is favored for fast and easy application. Some panels are meant to be painted; some resemble other materials—marble, for example; some are veneered with real wood.

Plywood paneling comes unfinished, prefinished, or vinyl-faced. Many natural and decorator finishes are available. You can also obtain hardboard products that simulate brick, stone, wood, marble, and tile.

Mirrors can serve as a form of architectural deception—they make a room look larger, a hall look longer, a ceiling look higher. Mirrors can also be used to add visual interest, to diffuse light, and to allow people to "see" around corners.

Request plate glass mirrors if you want them polished, and free of distortion. Foot-square mirror tiles will be the easiest to install yourself.

For more on wall treatment, refer to the *Sunset* book *Paneling, Painting & Wallpapering.*

Mirrors covering a wall *frequently give an effect of spaciousness you can get in no other way. Here a stairwell mirror extends an entry landing and lets you see up and down the flight of stairs. Architects: MLTW/Turnbull Associates.*

Super-thin wood paneling strips are designed for do-it-yourself installation. Some of these mini-boards are only $\frac{1}{9}$ inch thick, are flexible, and can be cut with scissors; others are thicker (sometimes rough-sawn on one side, smooth on the other) and are sturdy enough to be tongue-and-groove.

three quick-and-easy wall coverings

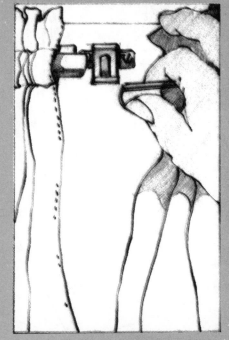

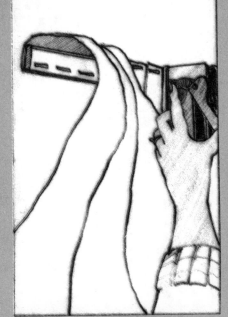

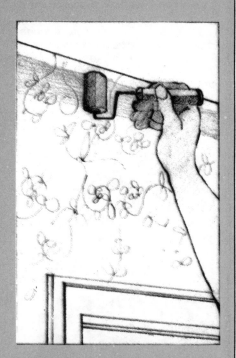

If you want to add a dimension or disguise structural problems, try gathering fabric. To determine the amount of material, multiply the width of the wall by two (for gathering); add 6 inches to each length of fabric for casings at top and bottom. Flat curtain rods, 1½ inches from floor and ceiling, hold gathered fabric taut. Consider using large, colorful sheets as your choice of fabric.

Flat fabric can be anchored close to the ceiling with a staple gun. First staple back of fabric through a strip of upholstery webbing as shown at left; then on the front, staple through all thicknesses to the wall. Working from top to bottom, stretch and smooth fabric against wall, stapling edges about every 6 inches. Fold under bottom edge and staple. Seams can be covered with wood strips.

Pasting fabric to the wall is the most permanent technique. Walls should be smooth and sealed with a flat, oil-base enamel undercoat. Roll cellulose paste—not wallpaper paste—on a section the size of one fabric panel; use your hands or a wallpaper brush to smooth fabric down and outward from ceiling. With a new razor blade, cut excess material against a straightedge after fabric is firmly in place.

Wall Storage

Storage space, or lack of it, ranks high as a reason for remodeling. Here, and on the next two pages, we concentrate on ways to utilize your walls—whether for a simple pass-through or as total wall storage units. On pages 90–94 you will find storage ideas specifically for the kitchen.

If you're debating whether to build a new wall or remodel an old one, make a list of your storage needs, then check the ideas shown here as possible solutions to those needs.

For more storage concepts, see the book *Sunset Ideas for Storage.*

It's neat and comparatively simple *to get logs from the woodpile to this storage space near the fire. The wood is loaded through a small exterior door that bolts from the inside. Armloads of wood can go directly into the built-in storage niche on the fireplace wall, thus preventing debris on the floor. Architects: Edelman and Lazdins.*

Bookshelves *that line a stairway can house a library with very little space loss. To avoid an unbroken line of solid books, consider including display boxes for art or sculpture. Pillows stacked on a stair landing will invite browsing. You'll want to provide adequate lighting, either from above or within the bookcase itself.*

Two-way win... ...pass-through between two rooms. The decorative diagonal bins are made of 1-inch wood stock. The depth can match the thickness of the wall, or if the front or back of the rack adjoins a cabinet, the rack can be correspondingly deeper. When depth permits, each compartment can hold two bottles end-to-end. Architect: Fred H. Field.

Storage cabinet that forms the wall between rooms is good for linen, art supplies, and utensil storage. Each shelf can slide out in two directions for access from both rooms. Shelves are closely spaced so that small articles don't get piled high. The lower portion of the closet is effectively used for vertical storage. Architect: Richard Sundeleaf.

Between-the-studs Storage

Have you thought of using the shallow space between the vertical 2-by-4 studs of a wall to add storage without consuming valuable room space? Framing into a wall and extending to, or beyond, the wall on the other side can give you extra inches of space to put to good use.

If you're planning to use just the width and depth between two studs (usually 3½ inches deep by 14½ inches wide), no extra support is necessary. When a stud is removed, though, you'll need a horizontal header above to help bear the roof weight. Check your local building codes. Do not use oversize headers with the idea that more is better; distortion occurs from cross-grain shrinkage, and the bigger the header, the greater the potential for distortion.

Here we show some examples of between-the-studs storage. Many more ideas may come to mind—from a fold-down ironing board to garden tool storage.

Bath towel rack can be formed by wood dowels or chrome-plated tubes that span the space between studs. Stained dowels or seamless, thick-walled steel tubes rest in holes cut in 1 by 4s that frame the floor-to-ceiling space.
Architect: Roger Kohler.

Those few cubic inches of drawer space you need for recipe cards, note pads, stamps, and other small materials may be found between the studs. Drawers like these can be made 4½ inches deep if you add ¾-inch-thick trim strip over ½-inch gypsum board.
Design: Alvin Lybarger.

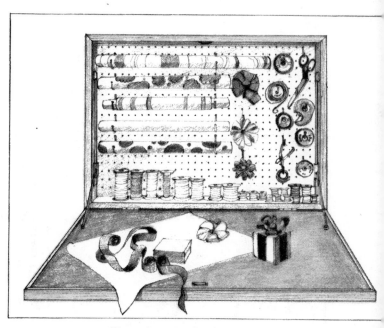

Wrapping counter *becomes a message center when it's folded against the wall. Pegboard, anchored with a frame of 1 by 3s, fits between studs. The corkboard front (you can also use chalkboard) is held at top with a magnetic catch; guide flap stays hold the counter level.*

Stud space *is used efficiently in the kitchen for food storage. Shelves, resting on adjustable hardware built into a frame, are just the right depth for spices and other food items. If studs are left in place, the exposed fronts can be capped with molding. Architect: Bruce Starkweather.*

Counters & Drawers

Drawers, shelves, cabinets, and counters are among the most important built-in items to consider in your remodeling plans. Use closed storage if you want to conceal clutter, open storage to display decorative articles or to keep objects that need to be readily accessible.

Even if the units are attached to an existing structure or stand in the middle of the room, they can be finished to blend with their surroundings. Built-ins can have camouflaged doors, invisible hinges, unobtrusive door handles, and the same trim or accent as the rest of the room.

For countertops, a tantalizing variety of surfaces is available. You can choose from a broad spectrum of colors, textures, and materials within an astonishingly wide price range. Here are just a few of the possibilities: plastic laminate sheets, plastic laminate bonded to hardboard, ceramic or mosaic tiles, glass ceramic, natural or synthetic marble, wood chopping block, and solid wood planking.

Drawers can be built into, and flush with, the wall. You can have cases custom built, or you may be able to find frames of chests that fit completely into a wall. Sometimes handsome antique drawers—or just drawer fronts—are available and can become part of a distinctive built-in. Drawers can open with pulls, knobs, lips, or decorative cutouts.

An oversize counter full of drawers can eliminate the need for overhead cabinets. The large unit eats into floor space, but the easy-to-reach storage can be viewed all at once. Even 4-foot-wide drawers filled with heavy china will slide easily on metal drawer slides. Architect: Lorrin L. Lee.

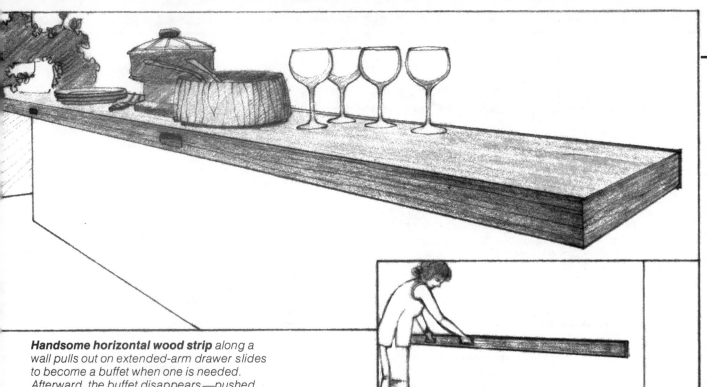

Handsome horizontal wood strip along a wall pulls out on extended-arm drawer slides to become a buffet when one is needed. Afterward, the buffet disappears—pushed into the next room where it is hidden beneath work counters. Architect: Donald Gibbs.

Package-laden shoppers can appreciate a slide-out shelf next to a refrigerator or back hall. This one is a simple box frame, using standard metal drawer slides; it's topped with a plywood surface and faced with the same material as the cabinets above and below. Design: David Clayton.

Safety & security

Remodeling time presents a good opportunity to inspect and evaluate home safety and security systems. Walk around your house, checking for security weaknesses; study your remodeling plans with the same thought in mind. Don't forget garages and other detached buildings. In some communities, you can call a local police officer to come to inspect and offer suggestions for security improvements.

operation i.d.

With an electric engraving pen (available on loan from some police departments), inscribe your Social Security number, driver's license number, or Department of Motor Vehicles Personal Identification Card number on any valuable property. If items are stolen, the numbers will help in identification. In a safe place, keep a list of valuables recorded as shown below, as well as photographs of small items, such as jewelry.

MAKE	ITEM	COLOR	LICENSE OR SERIAL #	ORIGINAL COST

CREDIT CARD	NUMBER

heavy hardware

The flimsy construction of many door locks makes it easier for a burglar, intent on entering a home, to simply pick, jimmy, or break a lock than to risk discovery by breaking a window. An intruder can be discouraged if the doors and windows are secured with high-quality hardware, longer-than-normal strike plates, and dead bolts or a self-locking dead latch.

safe entries

To secure your home against intruders and make it safe for guests, position bright outdoor lights near entries. Consider attaching the lights to a time switch or to a photo-electric cell that turns them on when someone passes through an invisible beam.

You might install a perimeter burglar alarm system at entry points. Space alarms are also valuable as a back-up system, detecting intruders once inside the house. Prune or remove trees, shrubs, or vines to open up landscaping that might conceal a prowler.

glass in your home

Federal Environmental Protection Agency regulations require that in your remodeling project you install safety glass (fully tempered, wired, or laminated) or approved rigid plastic in all hazardous areas.

Your home may have been built before codes covering glass safety were written or enforced. Maybe the best you can do is ensure that no one mistakes glass for an opening. Various devices can be used—decals on glass panels or doors; plants and furniture in front of them.

Along a glass-walled hall or gallery you might install a handsome wood rail as a safeguard to keep children away from the glass.

This decorative carved wood railing protects both people and the glass, and spans three window openings. Designer: John T. Jones.

in case of fire

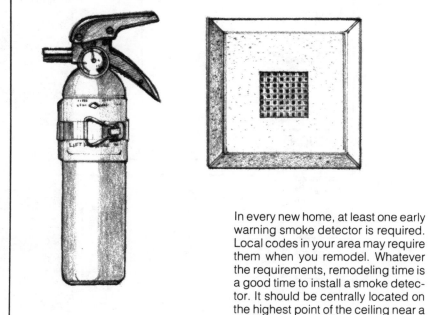

In every new home, at least one early warning smoke detector is required. Local codes in your area may require them when you remodel. Whatever the requirements, remodeling time is a good time to install a smoke detector. It should be centrally located on the highest point of the ceiling near a hall serving the bedrooms. Consider installing heat detectors as well, to provide early warning of fires near hot-water heaters or furnaces.

Fire extinguishers are useful, especially in or near the kitchen where flash fires may start. An extinguisher can be the best weapon for fighting a fire during the crucial seconds it needs to take hold before leaping out of control.

Choose the right extinguisher for the job. Household fires are classified into three categories (Class A—combustibles such as wood, cloth, and many plastics; Class B—flammable liquids, gases, and greases; Class C—electrically live), and extinguishers are typed in the same manner. To avoid confusion, the multipurpose ABC ammonium phosphate version is recommended for home use.

Door Types

Doors are part of a home's interior boundaries. The type or style of door you use often affects the tone of a room. Here we show some standard doors, and on the next pages are some one-of-a-kind doors.

If you are restoring a house, check first with salvage yards; they may have original doors from another era. The people who operate salvage yards are often experts in period style.

For all practical purposes, doors come in two thicknesses—1⅜ and 1¾ inches. To designate the size (width and height) of a door, it is proper to give measurements in feet and inches.

Door components vary with the design. Stile and rail doors have vertical members (stiles) and horizontal members (rails) that make up the framework. Hollow core flush doors have narrow stiles and rails hidden under a facing—a thin sheet of wood, plastic laminate, or hardboard flush on both sides. Flush doors are also available with solid core. Many different types of detail work may be added.

Areas containing glass in a door are called "lights"; any door that admits light contains one or more lights. In a door, safety hazard glass (tempered) is required for any light over 3 inches in diameter. Because colored glass is hard to temper, you will often see rigid plastic used instead.

For exterior doors, security is all-important. Though most styles can be used, solid core doors offer the most security and are often required by code. Steel doors and vinyl-coated steel doors are also popular for security. A wood door 3 feet wide or more should be at least 1¾ inches thick.

The finish applied to a door makes the difference in weatherproofing. Finishing the top and bottom of a door is every bit as important as finishing the visible surfaces. When you apply weatherstripping, it may be necessary to rout out part of the door—whether old or new. Be sure to go back and prime that part of the door before installing the weatherstripping to prevent later water damage.

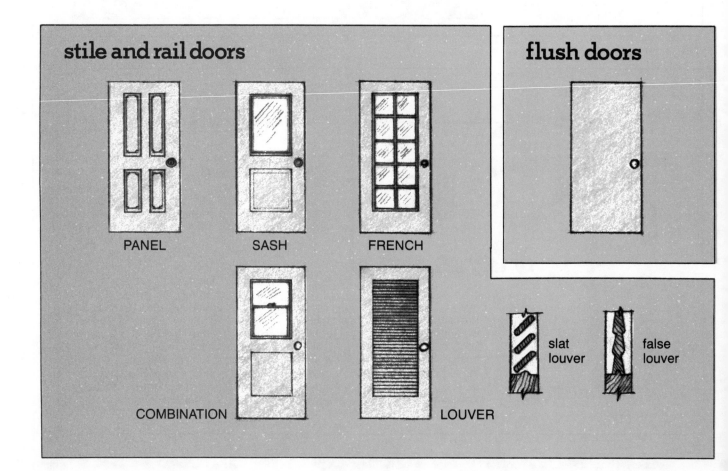

stile and rail doors

PANEL   SASH   FRENCH

COMBINATION   LOUVER

flush doors

slat louver   false louver

Front door intercoms and one-way peepholes (a wide-angle lens set in the door allowing the person on the inside to see out) are good for added security. Some peepholes even swivel for a wider view. A pass-through in the door will allow you to accept parcels without letting the dog or children out.

Interior doors that swing take up valuable floor space. Often a pocket door can save this space, since it slides into a recess (called the pocket) in the wall next to the opening. Pockets are preassembled frames with track and hardware that accept interior doors of standard size. The pocket requires no more depth than the normal 2-by-4 stud space.

In your area, fire doors may be required between any living space and the garage, or for closets containing the hot-water heater or furnace. A self-closing solid wood core door, at least 1⅜ inches thick, is the Uniform Building Code requirement. Fire-rated doors are also available and may meet your needs — look for the UL approved label.

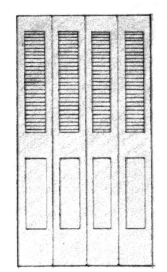

BIFOLD

DUTCH

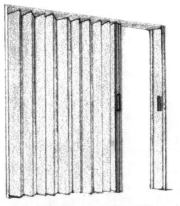

FOLDING (ACCORDION)

BARN

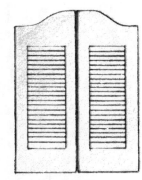

CAFE

SLIDING

BY-PASSING

Specialty Doors

The value of specialty doors is that they lend themselves to many decorating approaches and allow you to express creativity. This is especially ideal for front doors, often the first welcome presented to guests. And interior doors can be planned to make ingenious use of space.

Here we present some examples of nonstandard doors. They are intended to give you ideas about *different* doors and to start you thinking about how to treat these boundaries.

Almost any door can be enhanced by the addition of carved panels, or embellished with a surprising array of other materials. Nails might be pounded into a solid core door in a decorative design; a mosaic of wood pieces can artistically mask a weathered or surface-damaged door. Family designed and executed mosaic tiles, fired to rich colors, may cover a flush entrance door; a prized piece of bric-a-brac can be carefully inlaid into a door.

In a large room, oversize doors (unusually high or wide) are dramatic. In another room, a series of bifolding French doors can create a wall and then fold away to give access to a lanai or patio, opening the indoors to the outdoors.

On a smaller scale, don't forget to consider pet doors and parcel doors (small doors used where a full-size door is not feasible, such as a grocery pass-through from garage to kitchen).

Scraps of walnut, teak, and rosewood, glued on plywood and mounted on a standard door, make a dramatic entry. The wood is finished with oil. Design: Mabel Hutchinson.

Your front door can't be drab or obscure when it's embellished with a handsome, hand-carved plaque. This one was carved from a 2-inch-thick piece of Philippine mahogany. The lion's head was carved separately and attached with dowels. Design: Jerry and Kay Clarke.

56

Dramatic, attractive, and functional doors add interest to the homes they dignify. Rich wood barn doors (above left) roll on tracks to separate—and insulate from noise—two interior rooms. Design: Stephen L. Adams. Bright blue double doors (above) contrast with the wood handles and Mexican quarry floor tile. Architect: Stuart Baesel. Long, narrow hallways found in many older homes are enhanced with some focal point at the end—the leaded glass door (left) provides that interest. A circle of frosted glass above the door admits added light. Architect: Herbert D. Kosovitz.

Controlling Your Climate

Ideas for heating, cooling, and ventilation

Not just decorative, *this fireplace is more functional than most. The stucco exterior conceals a heat-circulating firebox. Cold air is drawn in through vents at hearth level, heated in pipes below the fire, and expelled through vents at mantel level. The amount of heat is controlled by the number of logs burned and the position of the damper. Design: George Silbernagel.*

Remodeling time may present a great opportunity to make your home more comfortable by adding to, or updating, its heating and cooling capacity. The first challenge is to keep the heat where it belongs—*inside* your house in cold winter months, *outside* your house in hot summer months.

The heating system will bear the brunt of any space that's added to your house in the course of remodeling, and the time to verify the heater's strengths and weaknesses is *before* the work commences, not after. Make sure the heater is in good repair and able to handle the increased demand of any added space.

Among many supplementary heating systems are portable baseboard heaters, toe-space heaters to install out of sight under kitchen and bathroom cabinets, and radiant-heating ceiling and wall panels with their own thermostats.

Weatherstripping seals the cracks around doors and windows, helping to cut costs of heating and air conditioning. If your house is not properly weatherstripped and caulked, you may want to include these items in your remodeling plans. And you'll certainly want to weatherstrip all new doors and windows. For more information on this, see the *Sunset* book *Insulation & Weatherstripping.*

Windows are a substantial source of heat gain and loss. You can limit heat conduction through windows with the use of double or triple-paned glass, storm windows, or anything (such as shutters and curtains) that will provide a dead-air space.

Glass with a reflective surface or a metalized polyester film (which can be applied to already installed windows) helps with sun control. The reflective sheen bounces back as much as 75 percent of the sun's heat and 82 percent of the glare. It also helps prevent fading caused by the sun's ultraviolet rays. For more on windows, see page 14.

Insulation should be checked in your original structure and included in any new construction. Look for insulation in the attic, and check under the house for insulation between floor joists. It's harder to tell if perimeter walls are insulated. You may suspect that they aren't—either by the age of the house or the feel of rather cold walls. You might be able to check by removing a wall socket faceplate and probing for insulation around the outside of the socket box—but do this only after turning off the power. You could also drill a hole in an inconspicuous place in the wall.

The building industry rates insulation by its resistance to heat flow—called its "R-value." The higher the R-value of a material, the better its resistance. The R-value your house needs depends on your climate and the severity of the seasons. Consult local utility officials, insulation contractors, or manufacturers for recommendations. Unfinished attic floors and crawl spaces should be insulated first.

Cooling a home in some regions of the country requires no more than exterior blinds, a cross-draft from open windows, or leafy trees that keep out direct sun. But where summers are blistering, you'll want to install air conditioning if you don't already have it. If you have air conditioning you may want to increase its capacity. And if you add more space to your house, your existing cooling system or devices may not be able to handle the increased volume. For greatest efficiency, consider installing an air conditioner with a precooling device.

Solar heating devices abound on the market, and remodeling time offers an opportunity to look into them. Consider the possibility of retrofitting—adding a solar system to an existing house. You might heat (or even cool) a new addition with its own *active* system (a mechanical device with pumps or fans, using water or air to collect, store, and circulate the sun's heat) or a *passive* system (the addition itself is designed to receive the sun's rays through south-facing windows; the heat is stored in the structure's own mass). For more on solar heating and cooling, see the *Sunset Homeowner's Guide to Solar Heating.*

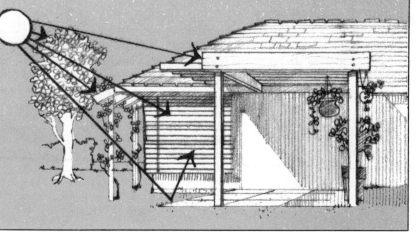

cooling your house

There's not much you can do about the siting or main design elements of your existing house. But there are several exterior cooling ideas you can adapt to block the sun.

Radiated heat builds up inside your house from sunlight on windows and walls, on the roof, and reflected off nearby surfaces. Shading with screens, trellises, overhangs, blinds, trees and vines reduces the effect of the sun's heat.

Heating with Wood

Few things do as much for a room as adding a fireplace or wood-burning heater. You may find yourself casually contemplating the addition of a fireplace; on the other hand, you may be remodeling for this express purpose.

Prefabricated fireplaces have some definite advantages. When a house is being built, installing such a unit usually costs slightly less than custom-built masonry. But at remodeling time, a prefab will sometimes cost only half or a third as much. What's more, it is guaranteed to work if properly installed; its relative lightness (250 to 500 pounds) eliminates the need for special foundations; and it can be installed in an inside wall or on a second floor (see some position choices at right).

You can choose from many brands, and the shape can be almost anything you like—square, oblong, round, cone, soup kettle, basket, tepee, igloo, pagoda. Literally, hundreds of styles are available.

Since any kind of fireplace is considered a permanent addition, a building permit is required before installation. And since not all prefabs meet code requirements in all areas, you should check with your local building official before buying one.

Built-in fireplaces are usually positioned in or against a wall. Available in different sizes from 28 to 42 inches wide, these units can be disguised to look like masonry fireplaces. You do this by facing them with brick, stone, tile, marble, or some other traditional noncombustible material. You can also buy manufactured masonry veneer hearths, surrounds (the mantel and side pieces), and chimney tops.

Freestanding or wall-mounted units are generally less expensive and easier to install than built-ins because the only installation cuts required are through the ceiling and roof. Most units also require a noncombustible floor covering and shields on walls near the prefab unit. Check local codes for hearth size.

Available in a variety of colors and shapes, freestanding units offer some advantages over built-ins. Their hoods and stacks help to heat a room rapidly, and their slim silhouettes allow you to position them in front of windows. This way seating can be focused on a view as well as a cozy fire.

Wood-burning heaters are being revived as a practical, economical answer to basic home heating needs. They vary in design and include such models as small, cast-iron reproduction box stoves; large, modern airtight heaters; grand wood-burning cookstoves that also heat; and elaborate three-way (oil/ coal/ wood) furnaces.

Most of these heaters have two advantages over conventional fireplaces: 1) They have controls for regulating the rate of combustion—a big, fast-burning fire wastes fuel and may actually draw heat out of a room; and 2) They are designed to burn the wood more thoroughly and to radiate heat into the room more efficiently. Fireplaces are notoriously inefficient in both regards. On the next page you'll find information on making your fireplace heat-efficient.

Be aware that in some localities home insurance rates may rise with the addition of a wood-burning heater. You might want to check this with your insurance agent.

The view beyond the fireplace wall may be worth preserving. Here the wall behind the fire is tempered glass. The reinforced concrete mantel, suspended between two piers, fits around a sheet-metal cone leading to an insulated flue. Since the flue draws efficiently, the glass stays relatively clean. Architect: Robert J. Swaim.

where to place the fireplace?

When planning for a fireplace, you have some flexibility in positioning. Fireplaces can be 1) framed into the room, 2) built in flush, 3) built in extended, 4) set into a corner, 5) freestanding, 6) two-sided, or 7) open ended.

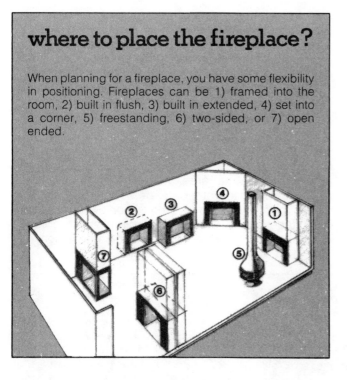

Barrel-type heaters, such as this one, come with tempered glass windows. Also shown here is an in-flue oven, one of several accessories available for wood-burning stoves.

making fireplaces more heat-efficient

Not all fireplaces are as heat-efficient as we'd like them to be. A roaring blaze in your fireplace may pull heat *out* of a room—heated air above a fire goes up the chimney, causing a draft that sucks up heated room air. This warm air may be replaced by cold air drawn into the house through cracks around doors and windows. When this happens, almost all the hot air produced by the fire goes up the chimney, and the only heat enjoyed in the room is the heat radiated by the fire itself.

Here are some ways to ensure heat efficiency:

In an existing fireplace with a strong draft, add a tempered glass screen with controlled air intake. Though this will reduce the heat radiated into the room, it will also cause the fire to burn much more slowly, thus drawing less heated air up the chimney.

Buy one of the several types of heat-collecting devices that circulate room air through a closed manifold system in the firebox and then expel the heated air back into the room. These operate by simple convection or—more efficiently—by fan.

If you're building from scratch, consider a heat-circulating firebox. Air coming from within the room or drawn from outside is heated in a metal chamber behind, beside, or above the fireplace, and then released (fan-driven or by convection) into the room through other vents.

Venting

Do what you can to insulate, shade, and heat your house. Then provide sufficient ventilation in the living area and in the attic to make your home even more comfortable and healthful.

The interior equipment you need will vary with the rooms' functions, the number and ages of household members, the ways you entertain, what you cook, and the amount of laundry you do.

In the kitchen, grease, heat, smoke, steam, and cooking odors are most effectively removed by a powerful fan through a range hood placed 21 to 30 inches over the cooking surface and ducted to the outside. Less effective, but practical, are ductless range hoods, wall or ceiling fans. The perimeter of a hood should be greater than that of the cooktop. In some cooktops, a built-in fan draws grease and heat down instead of up.

In the bathroom, an operative window, such as a jalousie, placed high on a wall allows vapor to escape. A fan above or near the shower or tub area is even more effective in removing moisture and odors. At least one of these—a window or a fan—is required by code.

Often overlooked is the need for a ventilating fan in the laundry area.

Poorly vented attics or dead-air spaces overhead can trap air, which can then heat to above 150°. This heat can radiate downward into the living areas long after the temperature outside has dropped. In an unvented attic in a cold-winter area, moisture can build up, condense, and cause water damage.

Shown in the composite house below are devices that offer effective solutions to air circulation problems. Naturally each home requires its own combination.

moving the air

1. ATTIC FAN, mounted in the ceiling, sucks hot air out of living space below and blows it into a vented attic.
2. CEILING FANS aren't really vents, but when they're combined with windows and interior vents, they can help move hot air out.
3. GABLE VENTS are inexpensive metal or wooden vents sold in all sizes and shapes. Tucked under the roof end, they are usually quite inconspicuous.
4. HOT SPOT WINDOWS in an ele- vated position can reduce heat build-up in houses without attics. Louvered or jalousie types make good vent windows.
5. POWER GABLE VENT is simply an electric fan designed to be mounted in a gable to force out hot air.
6. RIDGE VENTS (fabricated metal ridges with small louvers for rain protection) provide a continuous exit for hot air along the highest part of the roof.
7. ROOF VENT, usually housing a thermostatically controlled electric fan, can be installed in any type of roof.
8. SKYLIGHT that hinges or has a louvered collar can let in light and let out trapped hot air.
9. SOFFIT VENTS placed under the eaves are the best means of introducing exterior air to create an upward flow in the attic. Do not block with insulation.
10. TURBINE VENT has a louvered hood that rotates as heat escapes.
11. WALL VENTS are positioned high to release hot air or low to let cool air enter.

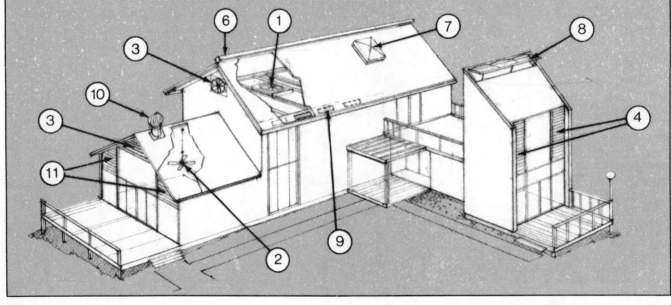

The living room of this tropical-climate house shares with a loft bedroom the luxury of breezes, space, and light. The tall, narrow window at left balances light, and its vertical jalousies open for ventilation. The ceiling fan helps move air gently about the area. Angled living room windows at right lift to a partially or fully horizontal position to allow breezes to enter. Architect: Chip Detweiler of Meyers/Detweiler and Associates.

Imaginative, Unusual ...yet Practical

Using alternative materials, from industrial to recycled

Before consulting a builder about new materials and remodeling costs, consider what alternative materials you yourself might provide. There are unusual and interesting building components around, and at a lower cost than you might expect.

Some homeowners go to wrecking contractors or salvage yards to find materials to refurbish for use in a modern setting. Or they may treat the recycled materials in another way, using them to remodel backwards to make a room look older rather than newer. Examples of rooms with recycled materials are shown here and on pages 68 and 69.

Other homeowners have turned to standard building components used in commercial, industrial, and public buildings. These modern building materials are simple and straightforward. They are generally not concealed or disguised but left exposed. For example, an electrical conduit left uncovered, rather than placed within the walls, can add a distinctive touch to a room—and the exposed conduit is easier to repair. On pages 66 and 67 you'll see more about industrial materials adapted for home use.

__Industrial stairs__ are a good-looking and practical addition to the area of this house the architect calls "the street." Two stories above is a dramatic glass roof that admits light to the area, keeping a multitude of plants healthy. Interior window at right looks into the study. Architects: Hobbs Fukui Associates.

__Wall collage__ of shapes and textures emerged from lath strips and a large wood crate, due to be discarded. The thin wood was attached to ½-inch plywood with roofing nails, their heads left exposed. A small leaded glass window punctures the wall with light. Design: William Shields.

Recycled bath *was put together totally from salvaged material. The tub is half of an old wine barrel, fiberglassed on the inside; the water spout is an old pump. Local rock for the walls and floors is complemented by beautifully weathered boards, and a skylight gives light to a potentially dark area. Be sure to check with your building inspector about using unusual materials. Design: Bob Helin.*

Small, interesting details *in the home may add that certain something you desire. Here, redwood lath covers the drawers of a cabinet, and the drawer pulls are big industrial faucet handles. During your remodeling, be on the lookout for items such as these—they're meant to perform one function, but perform another just as well. Design: Don La Lush.*

65

Industrial Materials

This brightly colored light tube is made of heavy cardboard. It's actually a concrete casting cylinder with a pull chain light source installed inside. The cylinder was first stripped of a waxy coating, then primed and painted.
Architect: William Bruder.

Some call it sculptural, others call it graphic—others call it unfinished. Whatever the feeling, it's functional. It's an exposed, standard-component, galvanized air-conditioning duct. The cost of framing-in is eliminated, as is the cost of registers—the arms have their own balancing dampers. Decorative clear-glass light globes in porcelain sockets add more visual interest.
Architect: William Bruder.

Several architects and homeowners choose to use industrial components in new and remodeled houses because of their simplicity, flexibility, economy, and functional good looks. They have found that industrial materials can be adapted to home use—both inside and outside—at relatively small cost.

Finding available materials and figuring out appropriate residential uses for them can be a challenge. Visit a department store to look at the building's components, materials, displays, even display cases, imagining how they might be used in your home. Examine new construction in industrial parks. Shop at commercial outlets, such as restaurant supply stores.

Some elements that may catch your eye are corrugated metal roofing, steel grating (can be used as an entry gate or as fencing), industrial sash windows, joists, and ducts. Industrial accessories include steel railings and stairs, sheet-metal paneling, restaurant ranges, dormitory furniture, flooring, lamps, and light fixtures.

You may want to talk to janitorial supply firms about product maintenance.

Look through the Yellow Pages of your telephone directory under "Industrial Equipment & Supplies" or "Roofs—Structures & Trusses."

A cook's work area is directly lighted by industrial fixtures suspended from exposed roof joists. Design: Andrew Beatty.

Some advantages become apparent when you use industrial components. Since commercial developers give high priority to keeping repairs and upkeep to a minimum, many components and materials are built to withstand heavy use with little maintenance. For instance, a floor covering made for a factory or dormitory will probably last a lifetime in a single-family home. It will also be easy to clean.

When structural components are left exposed—as they often are—the cost of applying finishing materials is reduced or eliminated. Repeated use of a single material can unify an entire remodeling project. Using too great a variety of exposed parts, however, can give a busy look.

Ordering larger quantities of fewer materials may allow for discounts. There may even be labor savings because of increased efficiency of installation.

Most parts are of modular (standard) size, which may result in economies if the parts themselves aren't too expensive. The components need few on-site adjustments in size, and the regularity of a modular design keeps down the cost of erecting structures.

Another advantage of designing with industrial components is flexibility. A room constructed with them lends itself to a variety of uses and effectively serves as a backdrop for many styles of furnishings and decoration.

Finding professionals to work with may be your first step. If you want to incorporate industrial components into your design, expert help is essential. Architects who do both commercial and residential work are usually the best sources of information. They know what materials are available, can evaluate structural and mechanical performance, and can figure out how to fit parts together.

Involving contractors early in the design process will also be to your advantage. They may help eliminate some building complications before the project gets underway.

Some challenges may be presented when you decide to use industrial materials. In some instances, you'll probably have to deal with special installation provisions. For example, building codes may require that a six-burner commercial range have a larger gas supply line than is normally used in a house.

The purchase price of industrial components may seem high compared to the cost of standard residential materials. But the durability and performance of components may justify their higher initial cost.

Recycled Materials

Finding recycled materials may be a snap. On the other hand, it may take months to locate just the item you're looking for. But there are quality materials and detailed handiwork from distinguished old houses being salvaged for reuse, and perseverence will undoubtedly pay off.

Wrecking yards are perhaps the first place to begin searching for old materials. Many yards used to be depositories for enormous collections of architectural "antiques"—everything from cupolas and stained glass to hand railings and moldings. Now the considerable cost of carefully removing such fragments has frightened off many of the large wrecking companies. As a result, saving fragments is fast becoming the exclusive domain of antique dealers.

Some dealers have agreements with wreckers to strip a doomed house before it comes down. Though prices are considerably higher when you buy through a dealer, they are still low when compared to the cost of comparable new materials.

A number of smaller wrecking yards have filled the gap between wrecker and antique dealer. The yards avoid keeping large inventories by saving only unusual items, but personnel will often keep an eye open for a specifically requested item.

Sometimes yards have extensive inventories of used lumber. The savings on such wood can be sizable, both monetarily and ecologically, and you also get the bonus of buying lumber that you know is well seasoned. A sandblasting company can clean charred or stained wood without structurally weakening it.

Some yards have their lumber approved by a certified lumber grader. If not, check with your building inspector for codes covering used lumber in major projects. Find out whether your house and foundation are strong enough to support any heavy wood or other objects you may install, and be sure you're not introducing termites or other pests to your house.

Another source of materials is a wrecker's "on the job" sale. Wreckers may sell salvageable parts right at the site of the house razing. A few—very few—will let you go into a building the day before it's demolished to remove fragments yourself.

It's still possible to find turn-of-the-century leaded glass windows, old post office boxes, bottle racks, and brass fixtures at flea markets, marine supply stores, and shipwreckers (check under "Scrap Metals" in the Yellow Pages). Look in a glass company's bone yard (a storage area for damaged, cancelled, salvaged, or returned stock) for glass replacements.

After you have the materials, there may be some challenges to face. You may run into trouble finding a contractor, architect, or carpenter skilled and patient enough to incorporate yesterday's building materials or fragments into today's house. Old windows are often skewed; lumber can be warped. Some of the older building techniques may be hard for modern housebuilders to duplicate.

But it pays to search for competent help. Once you've found someone who can make your plans work, the salvaging, sanding, rubbing, and cleaning you do will give a distinctive, personal quality to your home.

Using recycled details may be more to your liking than recycling major structural components. You may decide that a few novel items in your house could improve it.

When you see articles with good design, color, or texture, consider using them in your home as alternative materials. Play with the idea of making a sink out of a copper bowl, a wash stand out of an old chest of drawers, drawer pulls of sprinkler heads, door handles of prunings from your backyard apple tree. You may want one window replaced with old etched glass. By exercising your imagination, you can give your home an unusual and very personal style.

This porthole from an old ship is now used in a bath. The walrus was professionally etched for the new owners. Interior Designer: Carol Weiss.

Inexpensive recycled windows *were the start of this greenhouse. The windows were bought at a flea market, and the framing lumber came from the remains of an old tank house. Design: Doris Woods.*

Handsome arched window *surrounded by curved molding, now gracing a new entry, was originally in a schoolhouse that was torn down. Architect: William T. Hawkins.*

Entries: the tone setters

It's in the entry that guests receive their first impression of a home's interior. How that entry is treated sets the tone for the other rooms.

Because the boundaries of entries vary, it is difficult to set guidelines for remodeling. An entry door can open directly into the main living area, into a hall, or into a self-contained reception room. Entries can regulate traffic—slow it down, speed it up, divert it to an anteroom, or point it directly to the living room. Some entry areas, especially long halls, take on added interest when they're used as art galleries.

Don't let problem entrances defeat a remodeling project. If the entry is awkwardly located, consider moving it. Or enlarge the door area to make it more prominent. With a two-story house, why not design an open gallery-deck overlooking a lower level, allowing a sweeping view of the room below?

Having a coat closet, coat hooks, or umbrella stand within the entry area is practical, for family as well as guests.

Finally, there are two cautions we would make. First, be sure to provide good lighting in your entry. Second, make sure any stairs are well marked, easily seen, and supplied with handrails.

This glass-walled bridge, though dramatic, isn't just architectural whimsy. It connects a two-part house. The entry, living room, and den are at one end; the kitchen, dining room, family room, and bedrooms are at the other. In the open center is a peaceful, protected garden. Standard tempered sliding glass doors, installed to be permanently closed, form the bridge's window walls. The plan would be equally advantageous as an entry-passageway from a streetside garage to the house. Architect: John Blanton.

Clutter is stopped at the door if you provide drop space for books, sports gear, and packages where you come in. Each family member can have a divided cubbyhole unit. Architect: George Cody.

Once-dark entry is now a light, pleasant welcome to guests, thanks to a skylight that allows plants to thrive; gray-tinted tempered glass keeps out too-strong direct light. Track lights that once lighted the area from above were placed behind the plants to create interesting shadows and light patterns. Architect: Donald King Loomis.

Outdoor trellis is a transition from the open skies to the interior spaces of this house. Glazed ceramic tile hall and stairs draw visitors in and up to the living room. The owners had many view requirements, so windows were placed to present interesting scenes. The window at the right of the entry doors provides one of these views, as well as daylight for the hall. Architect: Donald King Loomis.

Room Remodeling for Special Purposes

Ideas for children, hobbies, plants

In previous chapters you have seen ideas that can be applied to any room in the house. This chapter and the next are devoted to specific rooms.

Some rooms become candidates for remodeling as the occupants' needs change. For this reason, parents often remodel a child's bedroom. On pages 74 and 75 we offer some suggestions for such remodeling.

Sometimes people who develop their hobbies after they buy a house decide to remodel to accommodate their new interests. Though the settings for hobbies differ considerably, you may find some clues to remodeling for your hobby on pages 76 and 77.

Here and throughout the chapter are photographs of some ways homeowners have remodeled special rooms, with treatments ranging from the simple to the complex. Some kitchen and bath inspirations are shown in the next chapter, beginning on page 80.

A simple solution to room remodeling needs is often more decorative than structural. For this home entertainment center, 2 by 2-inch wood strips form a grid on the wall for brightly painted plywood boxes. They are bolted in place through predrilled holes. A steel pipe forms a geometric stepladder.
Design: Richard Pennington.

Once an attic, it's now an attractive crafts room. Though the roof line dictates the space, it is used efficiently —under the downslope is a large work table, for which head room is not needed. A recycled half-circle window sits above a newer one, bringing light into the room. Industrial shades cover the lights along the roof ridge line.
Design: Don and Roberta Vandervort.

This simple tension screen serves as room divider, bed headboard, slide projector screen, closet wall, and part of the counterbalance for a clothes rack. To duplicate the screen, hem lightweight canvas at top and bottom to accept a 1-inch dowel the length desired. Make cutouts every 3 feet or less at top, and make two cutouts at bottom as shown (bind edges, or turn and hem). Attach eyebolts (A) to wooden clothes pole every 3 feet (or the center-to-center distance of the cutouts). Position a series of matching eyebolts (B) in a ceiling joist. Make a parallel series of eyebolts (C) 32 inches (or two joist spans) away—screen will fall midway between points (B) and (C). Tie a nylon cord to each eyebolt (A) in clothes pole. Thread first cord through eyebolt (B) above, then down through screen cutout and under and around dowel; tie off at eyebolt (C). Repeat for the rest of the cords. Tie and eyebolt bottom dowel to floor. Correct the clothes pole height when screen is taut; load clothes rack.
Design: Richard Pennington.

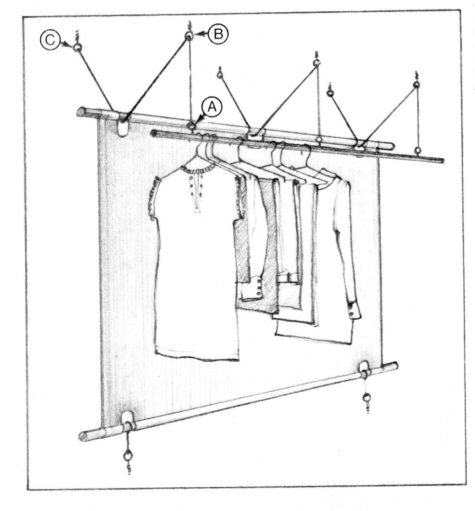

Space for desk, toys, and play was gained by
the addition of a supersize shelf along one end
of this bedroom. A 4½-foot ladder provides
access to the "second floor" sleeping loft.
Notched dowels projecting from each side are
handy coat racks. The loft is further accented by
bold supergraphics. Architect: Gerald Cichanski.

Pull-out beds beneath waterbeds provide plenty of
sleeping space in these children's rooms. Barn
doors, faced with ½ by 6-inch redwood
benderboard, close for privacy. Since the eaves of
the house were lost in the remodeling, low strip
windows were chosen for sun protection. Small
soffit lamps provide over-bed light.
Architect: William Bruder.

For Children

What fun for children when their room is redone just for them! Turning a room into a jungle, using bold strokes of paint to accent a print of a racing car, decorating a window seat like a treehouse—all these different treatments add to children's fantasies and make their rooms special.

But rooms should be able to grow with the children. A child, and your long-range budget, will benefit from changeable furniture. One old and valuable idea is a hollow-core door used as a desk top—children like to spread out, and a door provides lots of work space. Drawers or modular storage units placed underneath can be added to for height. As a child grows, so does storage.

Another storage idea is under-the-bed drawers. One large drawer on wheels can hold toys and stuffed animals—or even a whole train setup. When tired of being a zoo keeper or the train's engineer, a child can roll the drawer back under the bed.

Allow for space when remodeling—it's important for children. One way to free up space is to install a platform bed. A platform or drop-down bunk that attaches to a wall can be lifted and held out of the way with latches. The bottom side of a drop-down bunk makes a good bulletin board area when the bunk is lifted.

Raising a bed high off the floor gives room below for play and storage. A protective rail will prevent a sleeping child from falling over the edge. If stairs lead to a loft, they should be well secured.

The temperature around a raised bed may be higher than it would be around a lower bed; ventilation may be necessary. A small window placed near the bed will allow a child to adjust the amount of air admitted without creating a security problem.

Children who share rooms will enjoy privacy of their own. Creative use of partitions, movable or not, will aid in creating that privacy. An example is shown at right.

One playroom by day converts to three bedrooms by night. A folding partition pulls out from between the dressers, dividing the back room. The room in the foreground is private when the folding doors are closed. Closets and dressers provide generous storage space. Architect: Donald Goldman.

This miniloft, a bed above the closet, leaves more play space in the small bedroom. It was the youngster's own choice for a sleeping place. Hooks in the closet make hanging clothes easy. Architect: Weldon Jean Skirvin.

For Hobbies

A home studio is the dream of almost every person who has to organize and stash away art, craft, or music gear at the height of a project. To make this dream a reality, consider setting aside a room or portion of a room for your hobbies. Part of a room can easily be dubbed the "music room"; a wide hallway can accommodate the artist's easel; even a single wall in the family room can be used for a ballet bar; and an extra bath can double as a photographic studio.

Hobby areas reflect not only your interests but also your work style and personality. The kinds and amount of work space and storage you need depend on the hobby you are involved in. You might be able to get along with a cubbyhole area, or you might desperately need generous amounts of space. Some people tolerate clutter; they don't mind having tools and supplies in view. Others prefer the disappearing workshop—an area or room that can be made organized or clutter-free in an instant.

Whatever your hobby—wine tasting, gardening, sewing, or others—remodeling can increase your enjoyment of it. After stacked cases of wine crowd the clothes out of your closets, or a prize bottle ends up in a kitchen cupboard, you may decide it's time to add a wine room. Or just added wine racks may be a boon.

In this section we offer some solutions to the need for hobby space. For more on remodeling for plants, turn to page 78.

a room for your wine

When you design a wine room, give first consideration to temperature. Keeping the temperature low is important, but keeping the temperature *constant* is even more important. Visitors to your wine room can remain comfortable at 64° F. (18° C.) for an hour. If you don't plan to entertain in the wine room, you may prefer the more classic storage level at 58° F. (14.5° C.).

You'll need to insulate a wine room well, and use doors that are solid core and weatherstripped. For security, use a good lock. Choose flooring that is reasonably soft, so that a dropped bottle will stand a chance of surviving unbroken (a cushioned vinyl is good), and something that won't be ruined if wine is spilled.

A good wine deserves to age in quiet solitude. Bottles should be held securely and still be open to easy viewing; you'll want to identify a bottle without moving it. And plan for distance to protect wines from sources of vibration—furnace, air conditioning, even a stairway.

Make your wine room light-tight. Over a period of several years, sunlight and other sources of ultraviolet light are harmful to wine. But feel free to install artificial light to help you search for bottles or to illuminate wine tastings.

Diamond racks, each a 14 by 14-inch section, hold 16 bottles of wine apiece.

Central storage unit in this wine cellar holds a case of wine per vertical slit, with identifying bottles on top.

White-painted roof glass in this studio-greenhouse provides even, shade-free lighting for the artist and keeps the room cool during hot summers.

Vertical storage is best for paintings, holding them in an upright position so they can be easily moved in and out. Here they are kept in tall, deep slots. The front part of the cabinet contains shelf storage and is faced with a door that serves as a pin-up surface.

Ceramic studio with exposed rafters, plumbing, and shelves is remodeled version of an old garage. A clear plastic skylight crowns the roof; shelves are suspended from rafters. Architect: Lawrence Steiner.

For Plants

Persistent gardeners defy the seasons by surrounding themselves with greenery inside the home.

No rule says house plants must be small or must exist quietly in pots and planters. Some homeowners are making complete indoor gardens, providing them with plenty of space and natural light. One innovative example is shown in the kitchen plan on pages 90 and 91. A simpler solution is hanging plants (one way is shown on the facing page, top right) or caring for plants in pots (some display help is sketched below).

The house tree can make a strong accent in your home. Trees can fill in empty corners, be room dividers, and hide problem areas.

Before remodeling, consider the type of plants you want to nurture. Study their needs. Then as part of the remodeling plans, provide adequate light, correct temperature, and proper humidity level. After that, plant care will be easier and perhaps more fun.

Add-on greenhouse bays, *a simple window replacement idea, reach out to catch the sunlight. Top and sides often open for ventilation.*

Potted plants *fill this atrium-stairwell with greenery. Chemistry lab rings attached to balusters keep plants where they get most sunlight.*
Architect: Daniel M. Streissguth.

Artful display *of plants is suspended from a 12-foot commercial track that spans the ceiling. Plants can be moved around or changed as necessary. Plant lights supplement the sunlight admitted by the window.*

Greenery-filled *entertaining room with a clear plastic skylight was an addition for this house. Plants that can tolerate sun and heat perch on the center beam; others thrive around the room. Design: Errol Dierks.*

Gallery *in an old adobe became a winter plant room. During the cold season, plants receive light and sun from the south-facing windows. The rounded ceiling beams are traditional for adobe architecture. If your home has a broad overhang, you might consider enclosing it for your own plant gallery.*

The Two Most Remodeled Rooms

Bath and kitchen come under close scrutiny

Rooms that are used constantly tend to be remodeled, updated, and changed more frequently than others. The two rooms most often remodeled in our houses are the bath and the kitchen.

Here we present a kitchen and some baths in color for your enjoyment and idea gathering. On pages 82–85 you will find more on the bath. Pages 86–94 are devoted to the kitchen.

***Pleasant country kitchen** is the result of remodeling a "plain Jane". The old kitchen's dropped ceiling was raised, and walls and a door were removed between the kitchen and porch. (Now enclosed, the porch space provides room for an office area and wood-burning stove.) The parquet floor is from an old gymnasium. Architect: William Fletcher.*

An overall feeling of warmth comes from the wood tones in this bathroom. Cabinets are rough-sawn redwood plywood; ceiling and tub facing are of the same type of plywood, but with the addition of grooves. The countertop is oak flooring. Track lights allow the light to be positioned for greatest efficiency. Architect: Ron Yeo.

Floral sinks add a decorative touch to a bathroom. Here, hand-painted Mexican sinks, shallow but wide, rest on a slightly higher than standard counter. Look for handmade sinks in pottery galleries, and be sure they are high-fire glazed for durability. Design: George Silbernagel.

There's a Japanese-European influence in the design of this bathroom. The entire area was first tiled and a floor drain installed before the spaced cedar board floor was laid. In Japanese tradition, you can sit on the bench outside the tub and scrub down with soapy water from the bucket, rinse off, and then use the clean tub for soaking. Or use just the tub for a leisurely European-style bubble bath — propping a book on the cedar shelf. Architect: Robert B. Marquis of Marquis Associates.

Decorative tile, wood, and leaded glass accent this remodeled bath. Blue and brown tile continues past the sink counter, under a plant ledge, and around the tub. The original bathroom had a narrow entry and no bathtub. With the end wall pushed out 5 feet, the area now accommodates a large oval tub, and there's room for dual sinks. Oak paneling faces the tub front and walls. Design: Dan Rodriguez.

The Bath

In many a home the 5 by 8-foot bathroom has been considered standard. Recently, though, people have become aware of the shortcomings of existing bathrooms and are growing more and more discriminating about this important room.

Because the bathroom is frequently used, it can benefit from being enlarged. More than the standard three fixtures are sometimes included. In a return to Victorian style, baths are being compartmentalized—a good way to organize the room for use by more than one person at a time and still allow for privacy.

The standard bath, even without being enlarged, can be made to look bigger—or at least newer. Carpeting, new wall covering, new fixtures and counters, and better lighting can do a lot to update it. There are companies that will come in and resurface old enameled or porcelained fixtures with bright new colors—look in the Yellow Pages under "Bathroom Fixtures—Refinishing."

Glass walls for the shower will give a sense of expanded space; so will mirrors and reflective wallpaper. A corner sink saves space, and concealed storage eliminates space-gobbling clutter.

You can face an old tub with wood, tile, or plastic laminate and, at the same time, create a wider edge for a seat or a ledge for plants.

Adding a new bathroom presents many possibilities. Let your imagination explore some unconventional ideas. Consider including a dressing room, a sauna, a sunbathing bench, a garden, music, or storage space for reading material.

Though not always possible, the simplest and most economical way to add a new bath is to place it near existing fixtures, either above, below, or back-to-back. Tapping into those existing pipes and vents can really lower the expense, since plumbing is likely to be the greatest cost in adding a bathroom.

Some words of caution, though: Make sure you have sufficient water pressure and water heater capacity to handle the extra load. Walls will need to contain hot and cold-water supply pipes, water drains, and vents. In older homes, you may find that the plumbing will not meet your new needs. In very old homes, the pipes may even be the wrong dimension.

Familiarize yourself with local building, electrical, and plumbing codes. Since minimum distances between fixtures are set by code, measurements should be checked before you purchase materials and decide on a floor plan. Electrical switches should be out of the reach of anyone using the tub, shower, or lavatory. Ventilation—either mechanical or from windows—must be provided; see page 62 for more on ventilation.

If you are remodeling and plan to add a bath later, do the rough plumbing while the studs are exposed. This will save you a great deal of money later on.

The standard tub is given a face lift with wood. Molding and 1 by 6s frame the tub. The wood was stained dark and coated with glossy spar varnish. If you use this idea, be sure to carefully caulk the tub and seal the wood. Architects: Choate Associates.

Bath Details

Fixtures and accessories will play an important role in your remodeled bathroom. Collect brochures from distributors and look in magazines and books for ideas of what's new and available—the *Sunset* book *Planning & Remodeling Bathrooms* can provide inspiration. You'll be surprised at the array of materials—from full environment compartments that simulate rain, sun, and wind to complete prefabricated bathrooms that are lifted onto a subfloor.

Sinks come in a variety of sizes, shapes, and materials, and the vanities that surround the sinks can set the style for a room. On a practical note, consider the ones with built-in hampers. Look, too, for sinks that have pull-out hair-washing sprayer hose.

Standard tubs are generally available in porcelained cast iron, enameled steel, and fiberglass. Standard and unusual tubs can be executed in tile. But many people are also discovering what the Japanese have known for centuries—that wood feels good when you are soaking in the tub. Some homeowners are installing the traditional *furo*, a shorter and deeper tub in which you sit upright in water up to your neck. There's often a seat inside. Hydromassage units can be installed in almost any tub. Hot tubs that accommodate several people can also be part of the bathroom scene.

Consider sinking the tub (see page 42); or raising it—so much easier to bathe small children; or even encasing it.

When redoing a shower or building a new one, remember to provide room for soap and shampoo. Some prefabricated fiberglass showers have a seat built in. If your shower will be fully enclosed, you can change it

Two shower heads and a low spigot in the shower offer advantages. Turn on the lower shower head and you get wet only to shoulder height (not your hair). Turn on the upper, or both, for a thorough deluge. A very low outlet near the floor, controlled from above will allow you to test water temperature before diverting it to the shower head. It's also good for rinsing feet.

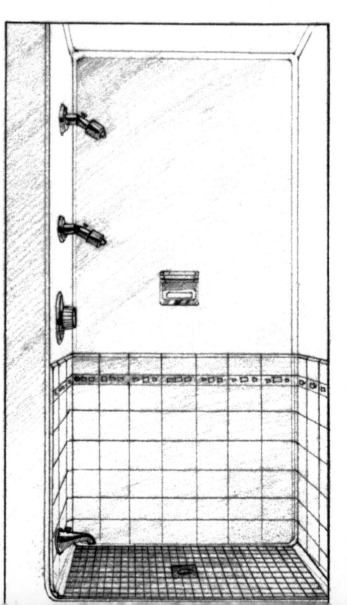

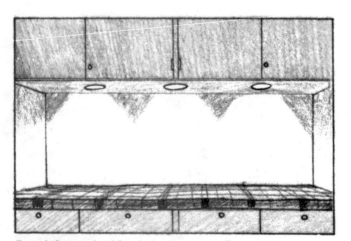

Bench for sunbathing *indoors was a refinement in this bathroom. It's simply a long standard base cabinet with a pad on top to stretch out on. Three sun lamps are recessed into the cabinet above the bench. Architect: Richard Sundeleaf.*

into a steam room with a special device.

A toilet can be made more attractive with the addition of a decorative seat. Also consider a toilet that uses minimum water. When planning the bath, don't forget to include on your list such items as soap dishes, night lights, towel racks, and cup and toothpaste holders. For extra pleasure, you may want to install a permanent or portable foot bath. Also include storage space for linens, tissue, cosmetics, hair dryers and styling brushes, electric shavers, and electric dental appliances. For children's protection, you might want to invest in a lockable medicine chest. Plans should also provide for adequate and efficient lighting, heating, ventilation, and sound control.

For more ideas, sketches, and photographs on the bathroom, see the Index.

Plants add attractive greenery to a bathroom. They take advantage of the humidity and heat given off during bathing and usually thrive there if the light is sufficient. The stepped bench arrangement, here conforming to a sloped hillside abutting the house exterior, gives extra room behind the shower for a generous display of plants. Design: St. Marie's Garden.

Towel racks are, of course, a necessity in any bath, and here is an especially handy one. The towels are within easy reach on a beveled strip of 2½-inch wood set out 2 inches from the edge of the counter. Architects: Akiyama, Kekoolani & Associates.

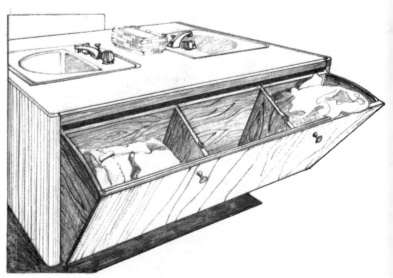

Three-part hamper drops open on the side of this double sink vanity. It's a good place to store and separate dirty clothes and linens. Heavy chains support the opened compartment. Pegboard bottom provides for ventilation. Architect: Leonard Veitzer.

The Kitchen

The kitchen—where families gather to prepare and sometimes share a meal—is the focal point of a house. Because of the wear and tear this room takes, and because of constant improvements in appliances, the kitchen is usually the most remodeled room in a house. And since it includes such a wealth of equipment and storage, it's usually the most expensive room in the house.

Different cooks need different kitchens. Do you want your tools on display, dishes within arm's reach, and food preparation open to family and guests? Or would you prefer to enclose dishes and pots, creating an everything-put-away look and a more formal atmosphere for entertaining? Cooks often differ in their choice of open or closed plans.

But cooks are unanimous on one point. Whether pressed for time or not, they want appliances, working counters, and sinks placed to help the flow and efficiency of food preparation. However comfortable and inviting the kitchen looks, it should serve as a sophisticated machine. Good traffic and work patterns help make this machine work.

The work triangle was developed in the 1920s by efficiency experts, who measured the basic movements involved in food preparation between the refrigerator, range, and sink. It has been generally accepted that these three areas should be arranged to form some sort of a triangle.

Guidelines were set as to minimum (12 feet) and maximum (22 feet) total distances between these centers, and this kitchen planner's triangle is still a guiding principle in kitchen thinking.

Today though, it is often modified. Appliance components have become separated—ovens are often separate from the range top, microwave ovens can be an entity by themselves, and food processors form a new dimension in some kitchens. And those 12-foot and 22-foot distances have shrunk markedly in many homes.

Logic suggests setting up separate areas or centers for different tasks to be performed in the kitchen. Consider arranging your kitchen with a refrigerator center, cooking center, sink center, preparation center, and baking center, with counter space provided at each. If space is tight, try a combination center or a kitchen island (see page 88). Locate doorways so they don't interrupt the work triangle and don't swing into work areas.

Many basic kitchen and storage ideas are presented throughout this book (see Index). The *Sunset* book *Planning & Remodeling Kitchens* is full of floor plans, descriptions, and photographs of good kitchens, and it includes a chapter devoted to details.

Do something different with your kitchen. Here we suggest ways—some in sharp contrast with each other—of taking the kitchen one step further than the basic work triangle. You may enjoy implementing some of the following ideas:

• Design your kitchen around a theme, objects you have collected, or culinary tool displays.

• Provide room not only for cooking but also for family eating, television, homework, and games; a fireplace can be the ultimate touch.

• Plan a very small kitchen. A tight size has the advantage of keeping everything within easy reach. By means of shutters or accordion doors, the small area can be opened up and put on display, then made to "disappear" when the doors are closed.

• Create a kitchen where people are zoned out of the way of the cook.

• Make the kitchen a place where parties always start or end up, thanks to abundant seating and counter space.

• Put all the appliances and work areas along one wall. Some people—and some kitchens—resist conforming to a compact work triangle and don't require an arrangement that yields peak efficiency.

• Plan a kitchen to accommodate two cooks, providing two planning, cooking, and work areas.

• Have everything you use in the kitchen in sight, either on open shelves or behind glass doors.

• Hide all the kitchen items away in appliance garages.

• Have the face of the refrigerator covered with wood, glass, stainless steel, or other material to give it the appearance of furniture or make it blend into its surroundings.

• Build a pass-through for outdoor meals.

• Have a steel plate cooktop built into the dining table. Then you can cook the way the Japanese do—with lots of show in front of guests.

Even with open storage, a kitchen can look uncluttered. The husband reports that his wife is "a magnificent cook and she wants everything within easy reach." Cooking is done on the restaurant-size range, and most dishes and utensils are visible. Some items—groceries, glasses, bottles—hide in the cupboards. The blue storage door is a pleasant contrast to the central oak work table, oak counters, and quarry tile floor. Architect: Robert B. Marquis of Marquis Associates.

Visual interest and memories blend in this open kitchen with its myriad hanging objects. The remodel began with a total ripping out of the area, exposing a brick chimney and ceiling beams. Old wood, stained gray to resemble barn wood, replaced the walls and faced the beams. Flea market pots and pans, a spice rack, a puppet, and other memorabilia hang from beams and pulleys.
Design: William Shields.

Small island *replaces an inadequate, narrow counter that separated the kitchen from the rest of the area. It's topped with ceramic tile, chopping block, and a built-in food appliance power center; the back side is used for storage. The island is also accented by hanging copper utensils. Architect: Edward Carson Beall.*

When the owners entertain, *everybody ends up at the generous kitchen island—and still there's room for two cooks. The 2½ by 11-foot island serves as a table for meals and as a work area for a restaurant approach to cooking. The suspended arch ceiling is made of 1 by 6 boards nailed to a plywood frame. Each board has a notch along its length which is painted black to create an accent groove. Architect: Daniel Solomon.*

Kitchen Islands

A kitchen island is often the key to a good kitchen, as well as the solution to kitchen remodeling. Installing an island usually costs less than adding or removing walls, and with proper planning, it can improve the efficiency of, or be one part of, the work triangle. In a large kitchen that doesn't have an island, you may walk many extra miles a year to prepare meals.

A kitchen island is also a pleasant place to work. Sometimes this is because of the island's relative isolation, but generally it's because of the feeling of space all around you—you're not facing a wall.

The island can be a small butcher block, a big cooking-eating-cleanup-conversation space, a place for the sink and dishwasher. An island can separate areas of activity and block foot traffic by acting as a divider, or it can be versatile and invite traffic.

An efficient island includes storage. One can be easily designed for your specific needs, with cubbyholes, drawers, and shelves to house such items as appliances, baking supplies, perishable foods, and small or large containers. If the cook is petite, the kitchen island can be built lower than standard counter height.

When an island is used as a cooking center, venting can be a problem. An overhead hood obstructs the view. A high hood can be used, but to be efficient it should include a powerful commercial fan. A range top that provides a draw-down venting system may be the best solution.

If a kitchen island is movable, you can have extra working space when and where you need it. When you finish with it, wheel it back to the center of the kitchen or roll it to some out-of-the-way resting place.

Butcher block island, 30 inches square, is stationary and has deep toe space. A flip-up counter, faced with plastic laminate, extends the work surface. Drawers on one side hold small utensils; the opposite side has shelves. Design: Harper Paulson.

Kitchen Storage

There are many, many innovative and useful ideas for the kitchen. We have compiled some that we found especially good and put them into the model kitchen— really the ultimate kitchen—you see here and on the next two pages. On page 94 several features are shown in closer detail. You're sure to want to incorporate some of the ideas into your kitchen remodeling plans.

1. Pass-through between dining room and kitchen
2. Roll-around serving cart
3. Serving cart garage
4. Cabinets with adjustable shelves, access from both sides
5. Storage for large pans
6. Food appliance power center in pull-out drawer
7. Flour and sugar storage bins
8. Lowered marble counter for pastry center
9. Appliance garages; appliances on boards with rollers
10. Flour and sugar dispensers/sifters
11. Semicircular door-mounted storage
12. Removable plastic garbage containers
13. Fold-out spice rack (see B)
14. Double sink; one side shallow
15. Dishwasher
16. High counter for breakfast bar
17. Shelf for cook books
18. Greenhouse plant and vegetable garden
19. Faucet, sink, and drain for indoor garden
20. Adjustable greenhouse shelves

See page 94 for close-ups of these items:
A. Removable cook book holder
B. Under-sink storage and spice rack
C. Corner under-counter storage

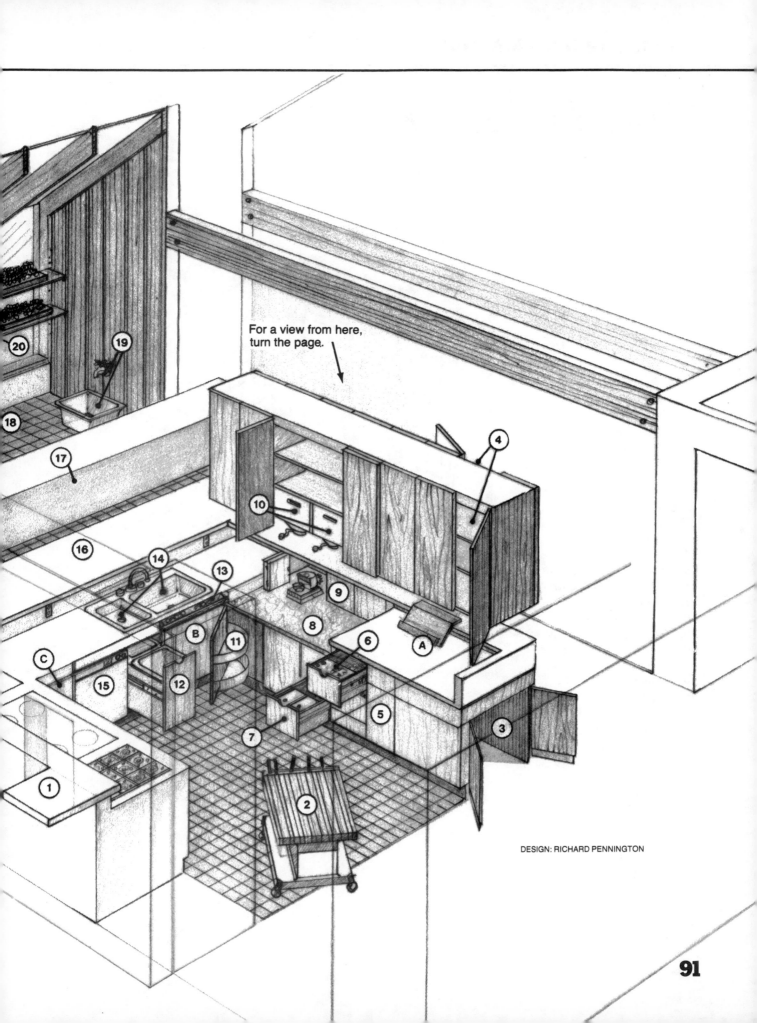

For a view from here,
turn the page.

DESIGN: RICHARD PENNINGTON

More Kitchen Storage

21. Cutlery storage
22. Family room storage
23. Shallow storage for linens

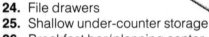

24. File drawers
25. Shallow under-counter storage
26. Breakfast bar/planning center
27. Garden supplies
28. Telephone
29. Plant ledge over cook book shelf
30. General storage space
31. Built-in hot tray
32. Cooktop
33. Trash compactor
34. Ventilating hood for cooktop
35. Tile insert near pass-through to dining room
36. Microwave oven
37. Toaster built into drawer
38. Lid storage
39. Built-in double oven
40. Roll-out canned food storage
41. Storage for little-used items
42. Dumbwaiter
43. Storage for large items
44. Refrigerator
45. Storage or laundry area with bifold doors
46. Freezer
47. General storage

DESIGN: RICHARD PENNINGTON

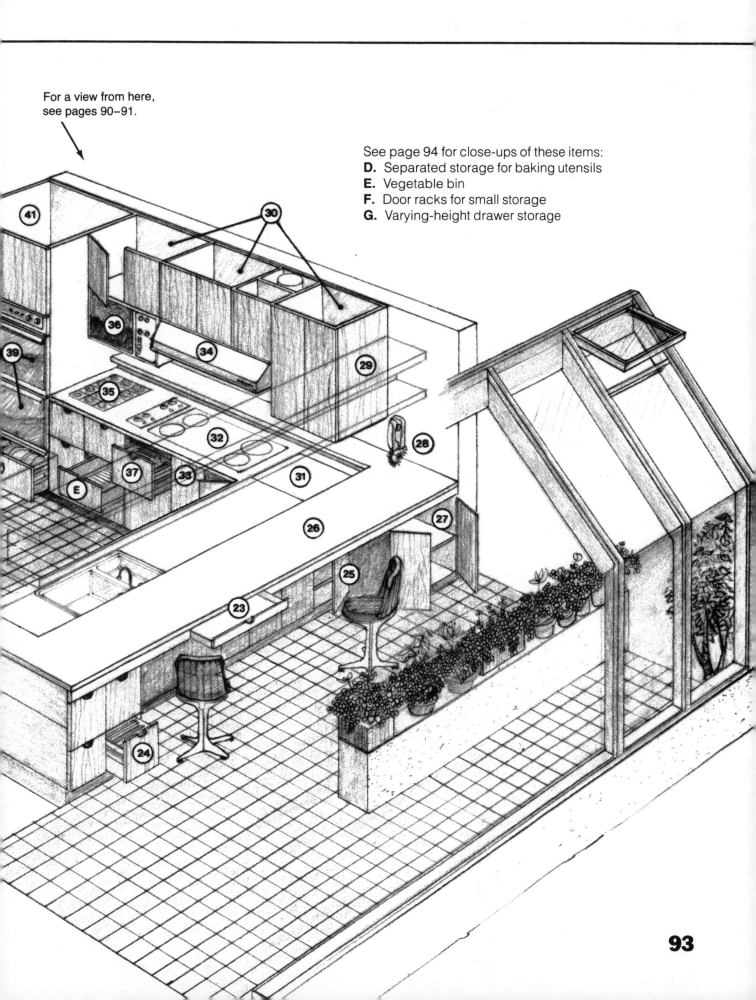

For a view from here,
see pages 90–91.

See page 94 for close-ups of these items:
D. Separated storage for baking utensils
E. Vegetable bin
F. Door racks for small storage
G. Varying-height drawer storage

Kitchen Details

B. Undersink storage has roll-out shelf for ease in reaching cleaning items; spice rack folds down.

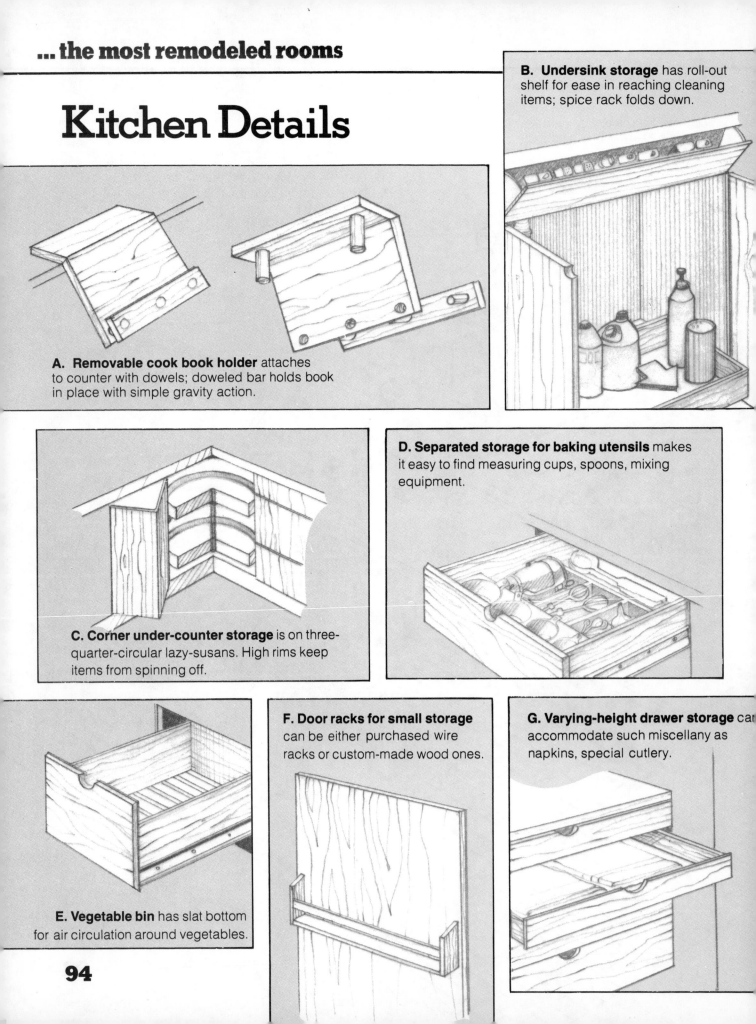

A. Removable cook book holder attaches to counter with dowels; doweled bar holds book in place with simple gravity action.

D. Separated storage for baking utensils makes it easy to find measuring cups, spoons, mixing equipment.

C. Corner under-counter storage is on three-quarter-circular lazy-susans. High rims keep items from spinning off.

F. Door racks for small storage can be either purchased wire racks or custom-made wood ones.

G. Varying-height drawer storage can accommodate such miscellany as napkins, special cutlery.

E. Vegetable bin has slat bottom for air circulation around vegetables.

Index

Page numbers shown in bold-face type refer to major sections devoted to the topic. Please turn to these pages first.

...index

photographers

David Bell: 79 (bottom). **Edward B. Bigelow:** 57 (right), 88 (top). **Glenn Christiansen:** 25 (top), 39 (bottom), 63, 79 (top right), 81 (top). **D. Gary Henry:** 9, 10 (right), 15, 18 (top and left), 72 (bottom) back cover (left). **Reverdy Johnson:** 39 (top). **Steve W. Marley:** 16, 26, 34 (left), 73. **Dr. John Marsh:** 82 (right). **Jack McDowell:** 57 (top left). **Don Normark:** 23, 40, 64 (left), 66, 74. **Norman A. Plate:** 17 (top right), 18 (bottom), 33, 58, 65 (top), 72 (top), 79 (top left), 80, 81 (bottom). **Darrow M. Watt:** front cover, 10 (left), 17 (top left), 24, 25 (bottom), 31, 32, 34 (right), 57 (bottom), 64 (right), 65 (bottom), 71, 82 (left), 87, 88 (bottom) back cover (right).